P9-DHC-417

WTF?
Work

How to Survive 101 of the
Office's Worst F*#!-ing Situations

Gregory Bergman and Jodi Miller

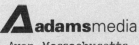
A **dams**media
Avon, Massachusetts

Published by Adams Media, a division of
F+W Media, Inc.
57 Littlefield Street, Avon, MA 02322. U.S.A.
www.adamsmedia.com

ISBN 10: 1-4405-0322-2
ISBN 13: 978-1-4405-0322-1

Printed in the United States of America.

10 9 8 7 6 5 4 3 2 1

Library of Congress Cataloging-in-Publication Data
is available from the publisher.

This publication is designed to provide accurate and authoritative information with regard to the subject matter covered. It is sold with the understanding that the publisher is not engaged in rendering legal, accounting, or other professional advice. If legal advice or other expert assistance is required, the services of a competent professional person should be sought.
—From a *Declaration of Principles* jointly adopted by a Committee of the American Bar Association and a Committee of Publishers and Associations

Many of the designations used by manufacturers and sellers to distinguish their product are claimed as trademarks. Where those designations appear in this book and Adams Media was aware of a trademark claim, the designations have been printed with initial capital letters.

pinball © istockphoto/mstay
nerd © istockphoto/Spiderstock
alarm clock © istockphoto/Rouzes
baseball mitt © istockphoto/Ju-Lee
fireman's hat © istockphoto/gregobagel
office freakout © istockphoto/PeskyMonkey
pillow © istockphoto/FineArtCraig
name tag © istockphoto/DNY59
paper stack © istockphoto/DNY59
mime © istockphoto/joshblake
polaroid hand © istockphoto/marimo_3d
wife © istockphoto/sofocles
map © istockphoto/grajte
whoopee cushion © istockphoto/Joe_Potato
flower © istockphoto/busypix
stapler © istockphoto/VisualField
masking tape © istockphoto/loops7
drunk santa © istockphoto/PeskyMonkey
office sex © istockphoto/Alija
condoms © istockphoto/MarieC2
VHS © istockphoto/Talaj
boss © istockphoto/sdominick
fired © istockphoto/tupungato
dog © istockphoto/GlobalP
ladder © istockphoto/thumb
cat call © istockphoto/kirza
vodka © istockphoto/oda_dao
$100 © istockphoto/hicksphotography
plunger © istockphoto/KevinDyer
patient © istockphoto/sbrogan
cigarette © istockphoto/Ljupco
sprinkler © istockphoto/ JimmiLarsen
whip © istockphoto/timhughes
dandelion © istockphoto/LockieCurrie
crutches © istockphoto/DNY59
goldfish © istockphoto/dageldog
mother © istockphoto/bobbieo

Certain sections of this book deal with activities and devices that would be in violation of various federal, state, and local laws if actually carried out or constructed. We do not advocate the breaking of any law. This information is for entertainment purposes only. We recommend that you contact your local law enforcement officials before undertaking any project based upon any information obtained from this book. We are not responsible for, nor do we assume any liability for, damages resulting from the use of any information in this book.

This book is available at quantity discounts for bulk purchases.
For information, please call 1-800-289-0963.

To all the bosses we have ever had for making us appreciate the beauty of self-employment. Pricks.—GB

Thank God I was blessed with a nice rack, which makes getting a job much easier.—JM

contents

Introduction

Welcome to the F*#!-ing Office

Work. To some it's the most vile four-letter word in the English language. To others, it is the very thing that defines them.

Whether you like it or loathe it, we've compiled 101 of the worst fucking situations you'll encounter in the workplace as well our recommendations on how to survive them. From sprucing up a shitty resume to dealing with a demonic copier that's out to get you to being caught downloading porn on your company computer, we'll help you tackle even the most seemingly insurmountable problems work throws your way.

In *WTF? College*, we helped our coed friends deal with the complexities of collegiate life. Now that you've graduated, we're here to walk you through the next stage: From getting a job to losing the job to getting another job to hating your life and losing that job to moving in with your mother and, finally, losing your will to live—

we'll be there to hold your hand the whole way.

Granted, life in a cubicle is not nearly as much fun as life on campus, but it does have its perks—like hot receptionists, happy hour with your moronic but entertaining coworkers, and, if you're the boss, telling other people what to do and making them feel like shit. Plus it provides the one thing we all need: A steady paycheck so you can buy shit.

And we know a little something about work. Before becoming multimillionaire celebrity authors (haven't heard of us? WTF?), we too had to slave away in jobs we didn't like. Coauthor Gregory Bergman has worked in various capacities from selling comedy club tickets in New York City to being an editor of a national financial magazine to performing private belly dancing shows at a Turkish bath house in Los Angeles. (He was young; he needed the work.)

Coauthor Jodi Miller is also a veteran of the workplace, having done everything from writing reviews about local carnivals to filling jelly donuts to selling imitation perfume out of her car on the Jersey Shore. (She apologizes if you bought that shit.)

So, you're in good hands. Now stop reading this book for free in the aisle of the bookstore and buy it jackass. WTT?

getting the job

1. You Have No Qualifications

People always say that if you do something you love, the money will follow. But what if you only love to jerk off and play video games? After years of school and thousands of dollars in student loans, you still have no useful, marketable skills. How the hell are you ever going to land a job?

The WTF Approach to Having No F*#!-ing Qualifications

➤ OPTION #1: *Lie*

Everyone does. It's the American way. And if you're not an American, then shame on you for trying to take our jobs. Get out and stay out!

➤ OPTION #2: *Go Back to School*

When people ask what you do you can always say that you are "in school." Now you have an excuse to be a loser, albeit an extremely educated one.

➤ OPTION #3: *Offer a Bribe*

Find out who is in charge of hiring and start sending gifts like pots of jam, fruit baskets, and whores—standard stuff. They'll probably admire your determination and hire you on the spot.

➤ OPTION #4: *Marry the Boss's Daughter*

Find the richest son-of-a-bitch you can and start nailing his little girl.

Make sure to knock her up to seal the deal. He'll get you a job at his business in no time so you can take care of her. Then, once you are bored with her, dump her, and collect half in the divorce settlement. If he fires you out of rage, sue him for even more cash.

How to Creatively Doctor Your Resume

There are ways to make even the most innocuous work experience sound more significant. Take a look at these examples to see how you can get creative with your past experience:

BEFORE	AFTER
Raked leaves	Landscape architect
Babysitter	Early education administrator
Worked at a fast-food drive-through	Food service manager
Planned friend's bachelor party in Vegas	Event coordinator
Chronic masturbator	Massage therapist

HEADHUNTER'S TIP

Positive action verbs make your resume achievements sound even more impressive. Use these on your resume:

- Accomplished
- Analyzed
- Anticipated
- Applied
- Appointed
- Appraised
- Approved
- Awarded

NOTE: You can also look up some *B* words, but we both know you are too damn lazy.

2. You're Over-Qualified but You Need the Job

You're having a hard time trying to find a gig that is commensurate with your experience. But the job market's tough. You need the work so bad that you're willing to put aside your pride and take a pay cut. The only problem is your stellar resume keeps getting rejected even for these bullshit jobs. WTF? Don't they know that this is way beneath you and they should be lucky to have you? Don't they know that they will never find someone as qualified as you for this position? Don't they know that they should actually get down on their goddamn knees and thank God that you would even consider applying for a job at their company? Well, apparently not, hot shot.

The WTF Approach to Getting a Job That Is F*#!-ing Beneath You

► **OPTION #1:** *Dumb Down Your Resume*

We've all lied to beef up our resume to make it more impressive (if you haven't then perhaps you should start), so why do the opposite and lie to make your resume *less* impressive? For example, if the position you are applying for is as an assistant, take out the shit about your managerial experience. Get creative. If you put your mind to it you can be working a really shitty, depressing job in no time.

➤ **OPTION #2:** *Get a Lobotomy*

If you are such an egghead that you can't hide your innate genius and über-developed skill-set no matter how hard you try, then you might have to get part of your brain cut out. Sure, you might not be the wittiest guy at the water cooler, but it's better than being the smartest guy at the homeless shelter.

HEADHUNTER'S TIP

If you do become a complete vegetable incapable of even the most basic thought, we suggest you apply immediately for a position as CEO of a major financial institution. You'll do superbly by comparison—just by doing absolutely fucking nothing.

How to Dumb Down Your Resume

You don't have to start from scratch. Change the wording of your responsibilities to make them seem less impressive.

Original Version: Spearheaded marketing initiatives designed to maximize company sales
Dumbed Down Version: Hired moronic telemarketers off craigslist to peddle inane product

Original Version: Able to multitask in high-paced environment with tight turnaround
Dumbed Down Version: Somehow managed to turn in work even though I spent most of my time making personal calls while I checked my Facebook account and planned my next jerk-off session in the restroom

Original Version: Forged key synergistic partnerships based on comprehensive market analysis
Dumb Down Version: I don't really remember what I actually did there, but I have references who say that I was good if you want to call them

3. Your Resume Sucks Balls

There you are hitting the pavement day in and day out. You are looking high and low for a job, any job. You have sent out your resume to over 1,000 listings. Not one phone call. So you decide to take control and call one of the companies to find out what is going on. When you get the head of HR on the phone, she starts laughing. "Oh," she says, "we thought this was a joke." Turns out your resume blows and even McDonald's won't consider you.

The WTF Approach to Sprucing Up Your F*#!-ing Resume

➤ OPTION #1: *Steal Someone Else's Resume*

Shit, you probably cheated off the smart kids in school anyway—this is the same thing. Ask to look at one of your friend's resumes then copy it. Or better yet, pose as a company and place a fake ad looking for the position you want. Collect all the resumes that come in then pick the most impressive and copy that.

➤ OPTION #2: *Buy One*

Go one online and pay a professional to write it. Or better yet just pay another kind of professional to rid you of all your anxiety—and we don't mean a therapist.

➤OPTION #3: *Protest*

March in front of the companies that won't grant you an interview. You might end up on cable news and become a celebrity—the voice of a disenfranchised generation.

Things You Shouldn't Include on Your Resume

- Violent felonies

- Weird hobbies like necrophilia or stamp collecting

- A nude photograph (unless you're really hung)

- A list of your favorite Polish jokes

HEADHUNTER'S TIP

If you still can't come up with some quali-fications, try beefing up your resume by adding *anything* positive about yourself. Examples:

- Non-smoker

- Good at pinball

- Tall

Sample Cover Letter—Mad Libs Style

_____
[Your Name]

_____
[Your Address]

_____ • _____
[Your Phone Number]   [Your Email Address]

_____
[Person in Charge]

_____
[Name of Company]

_____
[Their Address]

Dear _____ ,
[Person in Charge]

I am interested in learning more about and establishing my qualifications for

your available position, which I found through _____.
[Stupid Internet Website]

I believe I am aptly suited to work within your organization. As a

_____ at _____ I managed to _____
[Former Shitty Position]   [Former Shitty Company]   [First Lie]

significantly. As an employee, I am _____.
[List of Fictitious Attributes]

Finally, I am a _____ worker and believe that my qualifications
[Huge Lie]

and personal attributes will enable me to excel in this position.

Sincerely,

_____
[Your Name Followed by PhD]

Resumes from Hell

It could be worse. Your resume could look like one of these people's . . .

Adolf Hitler
112 Escaped Nazi Road, Buenos Aires, Argentina
Adolf@JewFreeWorld.net

OBJECTIVE

To attain a position in the genocide industry in which I can demonstrate my knowledge and experience in the extermination of whole populations from the face of the earth.

WORK HISTORY

STRUGGLING ARTIST (1905 TO PRESENT)
Self-Employed
Austria, Germany, and now Argentina
Painted amateurish watercolor landscapes of Jew-free meadows and brooks.

COAUTHOR, MEIN KAMPF (1923 TO JAN. 1924)
Eher-Verlag (Eher-Publishing)
Prison cell somewhere in Germany
Wrote poignant treatise calling for enslavement and/or removal of Jews and other sub-humans, as well as the development of a revitalized German Empire.

I am currently working on *Mein Kampf . . . for Kids!* scheduled for release this fall. In addition, I am working on Spanish language version for distribution in my adopted country of Argentina titled *Mi Kampf Es Su Kampf* (also set for an autumn release).

DER FUHRER (JAN. 1933 TO APRIL 1945)
Third Reich
Berlin, Germany

Accomplishments included:
- Killed a lot of Jews
- Killed a lot of Russians
- Killed a lot of Poles
- Killed a lot of Homosexuals
- Killed a lot of Gypsies

EDUCATION
High School Dropout
Austria, 1933

MEMBERSHIPS
- Future Fuhrers of Austria and Greater Germany
- Nazi War Criminal Glee Club
- Big Brothers for wayward (but racially pure) German youths

LANGUAGE SKILLS
German (and un poco Español)

REFERENCES
- Eva Braun
- Heinrich Himmler

Lucifer
666 Eternal Damnation Road, Hell
Devil@EnjoyYourStayinHellLOL.com

OBJECTIVE
To attain a position back in heaven; I miss it there.

WORK HISTORY

ANGEL (DAWN OF MANKIND TO FALL FROM HEAVEN)
Heaven

Performed various services for God, including acting as a messenger for His word. I admittedly lost my way and was therefore cast down from heaven. In my defense, I was drinking a lot at the time. I have been clean and sober now for over five millennia.

SATAN, THE DEVIL, SUPREME LEADER OF HELL (AFTER FALL FROM HEAVEN TO PRESENT)
Hell

Responsibilities included corrupting the virtuous, destroying goodness wherever it lurked, and generally fucking up the world and turning man against man to the best of my ability. If you want to know the truth (not that I'm big on honesty LOL), it wasn't that difficult.

Accomplishments included:
Jesus, where do I start? I have done so much over the last 10,000 years it's almost impossible to sum up. From famines to genocides to making that little bitch's head spin around in *The Exorcist*, I have had an indelible impact in human history. (I'm not boasting here—though vanity is one of the seven deadly sins and you know how I feel about those!)

Here are some highlights of my work:

- The slave trade
- The Holocaust
- Wars (All of them!)
- AIDS
- Investment banking

EDUCATION

Angel Trade School Diploma
Heaven, Dawn of Mankind

MEMBERSHIPS

- Satanists of America (duh!)
- Hell Health & Racquet Club

SPECIAL TALENTS

- Ability to shape shift
- Flying
- Can touch nose with the tip of my tongue

REFERENCES

- Adolf Hitler
- Idi Amin
- Bernie Madoff

4. You Don't Have the Proper Attire for the Interview

Dress for success. It's a phrase you've probably heard before, and if you haven't, then you're probably a poorly dressed loser. The first impression is a lasting impression, so put your best foot forward—preferably covered in some decent dress shoes.

The WTF Approach to Looking like a F*#!-ing Human Being

➤ OPTION #1: *Goodwill*

There's a place for schmucks like you, it's called Goodwill. True, you'll probably only find a plaid suit from the 1970s, but it's better than wearing your favorite t-shirt that reads: I Like Pussy.

➤ OPTION #2: *Beg, Borrow, Steal*

Not necessarily in that order. You should probably try to borrow first. If that fails, get on your hands and knees and beg in the street for change. If you can't get enough—even for a Goodwill leisure suit—find a way to steal one. Don't worry about the morality of it, you'll pay for it when you get the job.

➤ OPTION #3: *Get Creative*

Design and sew a suit out of your old pairs of pants. Wait. If you actually had a marketable skill like that, you'd probably own at least one decent suit already.

➤ OPTION #4: *Wing It*

Just buy a clip-on tie and smile, dumbass. Though it's best to be overdressed for an interview, if you present yourself with a certain confidence being undressed can actually work in your favor. It says, "I'm too good for this and I don't give a shit; you're lucky to even have me interview at this shit hole." Often times really, really, rich and successful people play it down. Just wear a polo shirt and khakis like some spoiled, "old" money, East Coast WASP and talk about how much you like sailing and voting Republican.

HEADHUNTER'S TIP

Just because it's better to be over-dressed than underdressed for an interview doesn't mean you should wear a tux with tails with a top hat. It just means that you should try not to look like a fucking scumbag for once in your life.

Dress for Success: Matching Game

Each profession has a different dress code. See if you can match the proper attire to its corresponding profession.

1.	Double-breasted Italian suit	A.	English professor and/or child rapist
2.	White short-sleeve shirt and tie with cartoon characters on it	B.	Conservative prick
3.	Corduroy jacket with elbow patches	C.	Mafia boss
4.	Suit and red tie	D.	Wal-Mart manager
5.	Astronaut uniform	E.	Astronaut

ANSWER KEY

1. C, **2.** D, **3.** A, **4.** B, **5.** E

5. You Oversleep and Miss the Interview

After months of applying for jobs you finally get an interview—and for a good job, too. Brimming with excitement and nervousness, you toss and turn all night in bed—alone and not in a fun way. It's so late by the time you finally fall asleep that you don't hear the alarm beeping in your ear. You awake from your deep slumber, rub your eyes, and look at your alarm: 9:00 A.M! Fuck! You should've been there a half hour ago.

The WTF Approach to Saving the F*#!-ing Interview

➤ OPTION #1: *Lie*

. . . but lie well. (It's a common suggestion of ours throughout the book.) Lying is the best policy most of the time in business. The truth may set you free, but it might not get you hired, especially when the truth is something like oversleeping. Here's the best lie to use: I was kidnapped. A lot is at stake, so go all the way with your lie. Draw your experience from *Ransom* and other films about kidnapping. Make sure to include in your harrowing story that your desire to get back to work, and to see your fellow coworkers, gave you the will to survive.

► OPTION #2: *Tell the Truth*

Again, we are generally against honesty, but if you really just can't bring yourself to lie, tell them the truth that you overslept. Then tell them that, as a good Christian, you can never bring yourself to lie. Some people really go for that shit.

Water Cooler Talk

"I recently overslept and missed another interview."

—Jason Jones, unemployed (but well-rested) for over ten years

6. You Show Up Hung Over to the Interview

>>>>> It was only suppose to be a quick beer then off to bed early. And you did just have one beer—followed by twelve shots of tequila, a bottle of wine, and two bong hits to wash everything down. After that, the party really got started. Now you are headed to your interview with a pounding headache and the taste of tequila and toothpaste in your mouth.

The WTF Approach to Dealing with a F*#!-ing Hangover

➤ STEP #1: *Boot and Rally*

You know you always feel better after you vomit. (Plus, you drop a few pounds.) Before you head to the receptionist's desk, head to the bushes and let last night's partying fertilize the company's garden.

➤ STEP #2: *Start Drinking, Again*

If your puke session didn't make you feel better, it's time for the hair of the dog, baby. Excuse yourself to the restroom, then run out of the building and find the nearest liquor store. Buy a bottle of whatever you drank last night and take a few power swigs. That should get you through the interview. Buy some gum while you're at it too, shit breath!

➤STEP #3: *Keep the Party Going*

Once you start to tank the interview (you do smell like vomit and tequila), break out the bottle you bought at the store and do some shots with your interviewer. Chances are they'll decline and probably either tell you to leave or have you arrested. But fuck it, at least you'll go out in style.

IN THE FUTURE . . .

Avoid hangovers; stay drunk—always.

Signs You're Hung Over from a Crazy Night

- Dehydration
- Dry mouth
- Fatigue
- Headache
- Sore in strange places

HEADHUNTER'S TIP

Make sure you get a lot of sleep before an important interview. If you are a heavy drinker, drink during the day and go to bed early. After all, if you're going to an interview chances are you have no job anyway and are a loser, providing ample time during business hours to get shit faced.

7. Your Interviewer Is Hitting on You

You passed the preliminary interviews with flying colors. You were witty, charming, and a good enough liar to convince them you actually know what you're talking about. Now it's time to sit down with the big boss for the final interview; the one that will determine whether or not you'll soon leave your mother's couch and get a goddamn life of your own.

From the start, things go smoothly. The boss—a super busty old broad with dyed-blond hair and a face like a saddle, weathered by sun and time—takes to you immediately. In fact, a smile seems to be permanently stuck on her face. Not only that, she starts looking you up and down, over and over again. Is she checking out your suit? Is she checking out your shoes? Or is she checking out your package? Wait a minute. Did she just wink at you? And then, as if there was any doubt about her intentions at this point, she lets you know exactly how she feels: Sitting back in her chair she crosses her legs seductively, revealing the most revolting bush since the 1975 December Playboy Playmate. Jesus!

The WTF Approach to Handling Her F*#!-ing Advances

➤ **STEP #1:** *Eat It*

It's a bad economy. Get on all fours like a dog and lap it up. You got to do what you got to do, pal.

➤ **STEP #2:** *Screw It*

If you want the job, then you better finish the job. Just be sure you do this Step after #1—not before.

➤ **STEP #3:** *Vomit in Your Mouth*

There's no point in telling you not to do something that you can't help. But keep the throw-up in your mouth. She may be kinky, but it's doubtful she is *that* kinky.

➤ **STEP #4:** *Smile*

The hard part's over. Nothing this job could throw at you could be worse. Unless this is how she plans to start every weekly meeting.

➤ **STEP #5:** *Cry*

Go ahead. It's okay. *Shhh*, let it out. Just be sure you're out of her office before you breakdown. Remember, it's not your fault. It's not your fault. It's not your fault.

WHAT THE F*#! IS UP WITH . . . BUSHES

The bush is slowly but surely making a comeback, like a patch of hair that was waxed a few weeks ago. Since the decline of the bush in the '80's—a revolt against the pubic hair-obsessed '70s—the shaven look has been the norm for women, from porn stars to soccer moms to porn videos about soccer moms. But lately, the bush is back—and back with a vengeance.

More and more the bush is popping up in porn flicks, like a neighbor who comes over for an egg and a blowjob. But who wants to see this shit? We know that fashion has a way of repeating itself, but the hairy bush has no place in the civilized world. You want to bring back something from the 1970s, why not start with the American automobile? Leave the clean-shaven pussy alone.

8. You Realize You Had Sex with the Interviewer and Never Called Her Back

You recognized the chick interviewing you immediately. Where have you seen her before? Hmm. You rack your brain. Those eyes, those lips, those perky breasts, that camel toe; they all ring a bell but you just don't know why. Then it hits you like a ton of bricks: You banged her after meeting in a bar and then never called her back. Now she's got you by the balls . . . again.

The WTF Approach to Lying to Your F*#!-ing Interviewer

> **STEP #1: *Play Dumb***

If she doesn't recognize you, then you're golden. Of course, this means that sleeping with you is not memorable, which is a bit of a downer. But at least you can avoid any confrontation. If she does recognize you, move on to Step #2.

> **STEP #2: *Make Up a Story***

Time to put those lying skills into action. However, we know how good you are at thinking on your feet, so here are a few stories to memorize for such situations.

OPTION A: IT HURT *SO* BAD

Tell her that you were scared because you liked her so much and you were afraid to get hurt. Then really lay it on thick by saying she reminds you of your ex fiancé who was killed in a tragic accident and that the one night of drunken sex—great as it was—brought up too much pain.

OPTION B: OFF-THE-WAGON ACCIDENT

Say that you were blackout drunk. Sell her on a sob story about how you had been sober for ten years, but fell off the wagon that night. Remember to reassure her that you are clean again and plan on staying that way so she doesn't hold it against you.

OPTION C: FLIP THE SWITCH

Tell her you did call, but the number was disconnected and you were so pissed and hurt that she gave you a fake number. Tell her that she really hurt your feelings.

When she begins to deny it tell her that you would like to be interviewed by someone else because looking at her is too painful. She will be so moved she'll hire you on the spot. Then bang her again out of gratitude.

for the ladies . . .

Here are the top five reasons why that guy never called you back:

1. He has a girlfriend.

2. He has a boyfriend.

3. Your vagina is stinky.

4. You don't know how to give head.

5. He is a guy.

9. You Can't Control Your Erection During the Interview

You're not sure why but something keeps popping up during your job interview and it's not your unimpressive resume. It's your dick. And you're not the only one that notices. You really, really shouldn't have worn your favorite skin-tight white suit.

The WTF Approach to Dealing with Your Raging F*#!-ing Hard-on

> **OPTION #1:** *Take Care of Business*

Excuse yourself to the bathroom and whack off. If it's already fully hard it shouldn't take long.

> **OPTION #2:** *Show and Tell*

Show it off and explain that even under these circumstances you are able to go on with the interview. This shows you have determination, and are able to work under stressful situations. If you really want to impress them, whip it out and start jerking off during the interview, illustrating your uncanny ability to multitask.

> **OPTION #3:** *Ignore It*

Start talking about the war in the Middle East, that should bring it down. If it actually turns you on more instead, you should really seek some serious counseling.

Thoughts That Cause an Erection

- Angelina Jolie, pregnant, holding a Third-World baby

- A crisp hundred dollar bill

- Coauthor Jodi Miller naked on the back of a tiger

for the ladies . . .

If you get an erection during an interview, see a doctor immediately. Trust us; you have a much bigger problem.

Top Interview Questions

Here's the heads up on some questions that frequently come up during interviews. Do your best to match the right answers—not the wrong ones.

What are your strengths and weaknesses?

Right Answer: My strengths are multitasking, organization, and the ability to work closely with a team toward a common goal. Hmm . . . weaknesses? I guess I am a perfectionist.

Wrong Answer: My strengths are my large testicles (both metaphorical and literal), my ability to take credit for other people's work, and my ability to bed multiple-coworkers simultaneously (Again, the large balls are a factor here.)

Why should we hire you?

Right Answer: Because I bring extensive experience, knowledge, and an actual working brain to your organization.

Wrong Answer: Because I am assuming that you value your life and the life of your children.

Why do you want to work here?

Right Answer: Because I have loved the pencil-making industry since I was a boy. I like graphite.

Wrong Answer: I don't.

What are your goals?

Right Answer: To work here like a dog until I die.

Wrong Answer: To be loved—by you.

Why did you leave (or why are you leaving) your job?

Right Answer: Because I did not feel challenged enough.

Wrong Answer: What job?

When were you most satisfied in your job?

Right Answer: When I knew that I had increased the company's bottom line.

Wrong Answer: When I replaced the water in the water cooler with a mixture of water, urine, and ejaculate. Ha, ha, ha!

What can you do for us that other candidates can't?

Right Answer: Work longer hours for less pay until my back literally breaks in half.

Wrong Answer: Blow you . . . really, really well.

If you could be an animal, what would you be?

Right Answer: I can only choose one? I love animals so much . . .

Wrong Answer: Who are you Barbara fucking Walters?

10. You Make a Bad Joke and Insult the Interviewer

Interviews can be nerve wracking. You hope to say the right things, look like a nice guy, and either have the qualifications or the bullshit capacity to fake your way through it. Making a joke is a great icebreaker in stressful situations, so when you get nervous during your interview and whip out your favorite Polack-having-sex-with-a-nun joke you assume you will ease the tension. Unfortunately, the person interviewing you is Polish—and her sister is a nun!

The WTF Approach to Covering Your F*#!-ing Ass

➤ OPTION #1: *Lie*

Tell her your sister was also a nun and was killed by a Polish mugger, and your therapist suggested you start telling jokes to deal with the pain. Hey, standup is cheaper than therapy.

➤ OPTION #2: *Start Crying*

Cry and beg for forgiveness like the dog that you are.

➤ OPTION #3: *Own It*

Hey, a good comic owns his jokes. Fuck her if she doesn't like it. If you think it's funny then don't apologize. In fact, break out another

Polack joke and then educate her on the need for laughter in such an awful world.

IN THE FUTURE . . .

Be funny.

Offensive Jokes

- What do you call two Mexicans playing basketball? Juan on Juan.

- What's the hardest part about rollerblading? Telling your dad you're gay.

- What do you get when you put fifty lesbians and fifty politicians in a room together? 100 people who don't do dick.

- Why can't white men jump? They were too busy making racist jokes.

NOTE: *WTF?* is not responsible for the potential jobs lost if and when you break one of these jokes out during the interview.

Our Favorite Joke

Two Jewish guys are driving around one day and they pass by a Protestant Church with a big sign on the door that reads: $1,000 to Convert.

The two Jews stop cold. Avi, the driver, says to Ira, the passenger: "Go in there and check it out. I mean, hey, a thousand bucks is a thousand bucks."

Ira gets out of the car and enters the church. A couple hours go by and he finally leaves the church and gets in the car.

"Well, did you get the money?" asks Avi. "Did you convert?"

Ira looks at his friend. "Jesus, is that *all* you people think about?"

11. You Can't Stop Staring at Your Interviewer's Massive Deformity

They liked your resume. The preliminary phone interview went well. And now you're in the door. Yes, you are just a smile and a handshake away from getting the job. But before you can charm your new boss into hiring you, you'll have to get through the first level of interviews with the HR person. But there's one problem. This "person" might not even be a person at all. She is a monster with a face so deformed she looks like the singer Seal had a baby with an actual seal—and then that baby's neck threw up. Whatever you do, don't stare or she'll catch you. Shit, you already did! Did she notice? She *must* have; you stared right at it. Shit, you looked again! What the fuck is that thing?!

The WTF Approach to Dealing with a F*#!-ing Repulsive Deformity

> ➤ STEP #1: *Keep Eye Contact*

Look your interviewer directly in the eyes. You should be doing this anyway in order to appear confident and build a rapport with the grossly disfigured pig-person.

➤ STEP #2: *Blur Your Vision*

If you make a slight adjustment to your vision to make the beast appear out of focus and fuzzy, it might help you stop staring at her monstrous deformity. Make sure you don't cross your eyes, however, or you will be the one that appears the most freakish.

➤ STEP #3: *Think of* **Schindler's List**

If you are on the verge of laughter and you can't seem to control it, think of the most depressing scene from the most depressing movie ever. Liam Neeson's departure from the factory at the end *of Schindler's List* is a good one, when he breaks down and realizes that he could have saved more lives. (If you actually *were* in the Holocaust, then you probably have an even more depressing scene of your own to recall.)

➤ STEP #4: *Compliment It*

If it is too late and you are certain that she saw you staring, compliment the interviewer on whatever disgusting disfigurement she has. If it's a big fat hairy mole, tell her she has a beauty mark that reminds you of Cindy Crawford. If it's a scar, tell her it makes her look exotic and dangerous. If she's a severely scarred burn victim, tell her that you used to want to be a fireman when you were a kid.

What Not to Say

Interviewer: So do you consider yourself to be a team player?

Interviewee: Yo, what the fuck is on your face? That's nasty.

Hierarchy of Disgusting Attributes and their Corresponding Affect

Not all ugly features are equal. See below for what to expect when encountering these heinous attributes.

LEAST DISTRACTING ↑	Crooked teeth	Mildly distracting if person smiles a lot
	Large snot hanging from nose	Distracting
	Giant zit ready to burst	Very distracting
	Hair lip	Repulsive, sad, and impossible not to look at
	Massive burn scars	Even more repulsive and sad because you imagine what she looked like before she was a monster
MOST DISTRACTING ↓	Missing an eye	Funny, like a pirate

chapter two

office
orientation

12. You Realize You Have No Idea What You're Doing

Well, you bullshitted your way through the interview process, got the salary you asked for, and have now started your new job. There's only one problem: You have no fucking clue what you are doing.

The WTF Approach to Getting a F*#!-ing Clue

➤ **OPTION #1: *Stare at the Screen***

That's it, just like that. Eventually it'll come to you.

➤ **OPTION #2: *Fake It 'til You Make It***

Just look around and start spying on what your coworkers are doing, and then follow suit. Ask questions like, "Hey I notice you finish your projects so quickly, what's your secret?" Someone might be willing to share.

➤ **OPTION #3: *Start Screwing a Smart Female Coworker***

Find a girl who appears to have no life outside of work. She's probably so desperate she'll bang anyone. As you two get closer, bring up the fact that you're slightly overwhelmed at work. If you are decent in bed she'll be more than willing to help, mostly because she doesn't want you to get fired—even she doesn't like to bang the unemployed. You might not only keep your job, but you may even get a promotion.

Successful People Who Had No Fucking Clue

- President Bush #1
- President Bush #2
- Keanu Reeves
- Sarah Palin
- Paris Hilton
- *WTF? Work* authors Gregory Bergman and Jodi Miller

Are You Good at Your Job?

Take this quiz to find out!

1. When you are given an assignment, you . . .

   A. Get right on it like a fly on shit.

   B. Ask a million questions like a dumb fuck.

   C. Rock back and forth at your desk, tears streaming down your face.

2. When you asked your boss for a raise, he . . .

   A. Took it as a joke.

   B. Fired you on principal.

   C. Told you to drop dead— and then fired you.

3. When you finish a project, you . . .

   A. Pat yourself on the back for a job well done.

   B. Pat your colleague on the back for a job well done.

   C. Wonder how the fuck they missed the fact that you totally suck.

ANSWER KEY

1. If you answered:
   A. You rock, keep up the good work.
   B. You might need some caffeine to kick-start your less than average intelligence.
   C. You are a complete fucktard.

2. If you answered:
   A. You suck.
   B. You really suck.
   C. You really suck and also have a bad personality—people hate you.

3. If you answered:
   A. Good work, attaboy!
   B. Looks like you owe some putz a beer.
   C. You are a complete fucktard, fucktard.

13. The Person in the Cubicle Next to You Smells like Ass

Every day it's the same thing. You're stuck in a 4' × 4' cubicle for eight hours. That's bad enough. Now add the fact that the person in the next cell smells like a steaming pile of shit and you have all the makings of a murder/suicide situation. But before you do that, follow these Steps . . .

The WTF Approach to Being a F*#!-ing Team Player

➤ STEP #1: *Go to HR*

Explain that the smell of ass, halitosis, and ball sweat is impairing the quality of your work. If they refuse to do anything, then send your smelly coworker down for a visit. Once they get a whiff of Mr. Shit Muppet they should reconsider.

➤ STEP #2: *Organize an Intervention*

If the pricks in HR refuse to help, it's time to take matters into your own hands. Get a couple of like-minded coworkers together and take Mr. Poop Bucket out for a drink (if you can stand it) and explain to him that no one will ever love him if he smells like road kill.

➤ STEP #3: *Out Stink Him*

When he rebuffs your intervention, it's time to fight fire with fire or in this case, shit with shit. Stop showering and using deodorant. If it's really bad, piss yourself every chance you get and wipe your ass with your hand. Show Mr. Stank Ass that two can play at this game.

➤ STEP #4: *Hose Him Down*

If he still won't clean himself, do it for him. Bring in a hose and start spraying him like a dog or a child from the Third World. Treat this like a nuclear waste emergency. Careful, don't touch him.

for the ladies . . .

If you stink, you should be shot. Women are supposed to smell like flowers, not fertilizer. If you just can't stop the stink, move to India. Compared to those people you'll smell like Coco Chanel.

WTF: UP CLOSE AND PERSONAL

In high school, a foreign exchange student from Russia named Artoom (most certainly the wrong spelling, but who gives a shit?) lived with us for a few months. On the first day, my mother bought him deodorant due to his repulsive stench. When I walked into my room and met him for the first time, he was putting the deodorant all over his neck and back. Yummy. I walked up to him, took it out of his hand and pointed to my armpits. "Just here," I told him, and walked out. Fucking animal.

—GB

Worst Smelling Places	*Best Smelling Places*
• Slaughter house	• Florist
• Porta-potty	• KFC
• Chinatown	• Medical marijuana dispensary

14. You Download Porn and Spread a Virus Throughout the Office Network

We all surf the Net at work. It really can't be helped. After all, do they honestly expect us to be working all the time? Occasionally updating your Facebook page is one thing; drooling over hardcore midget porn all day is something else. So when you decided to download the latest in sexual deviant behavior you also downloaded something else: a virus that infected the entire computer system at your company.

The WTF Approach to Covering Your F*#!-ing Ass

➤ **OPTION #1: *Play Dumb***

Explain that you were tricked. We've all run into pop-up ads: "Hey, look at this!" or "Do you remember me?" or "Would you like to see a co-ed blow a horse?" Seriously, how could you possibly know it was a porn link?

➤ **OPTION #2: *Blame Your Assistant***

That's what they're for. Tell everyone he's a big time perv and get him canned.

➤ OPTION #3: *Deny It*

Sure it came from your computer but no one saw you doing it, right? Pretend to be outraged. Scream things like, "Jesus save us!" while making the sign of the cross. Then only download your tranny porn in the privacy of your home.

TOP PORN SITES

These are some of the filthiest, most morally questionable websites:

- YouPorn.com
- Xnxx.com
- FoxNews.com

Tranny Porn: Gay or Not Gay?

If you watch tranny porn and are wondering if that makes you gay, don't fret—there's a good chance you are even straighter than your buddies.

Here's how the argument breaks down: A tranny is like 50 percent male and 50 percent female. Cer-

tainly, a tranny is *more* female than a regular guy since she has fake tits and makeup. So, if you watch a tranny have sex with a girl (100 percent female), then you are really watching 25 percent male action and 75 percent female action. Now consider regular heterosexual porn between a regular guy and a regular girl—which is 50 percent male and 50 percent female action. That means that watching a guy and a girl bang is *more* gay than watching a tranny with another woman.

Now, if you watch a tranny screw a regular dude, that's 75 percent male and 25 percent female. In that case, you're fucking gay.

15. You Lock Yourself in the Bathroom

There you are, taking your afternoon dump, trying hard to think of things to do other than work. You finish up, wash up (hopefully), and start to leave, only to discover that you can't get out! You are locked inside the bathroom, and the stench of your massive shit is making you dizzy.

The WTF Approach to Getting Out of the F*#!-ing Can

➤ STEP #1: *Start Screaming*

Yell for help as you bang on the door. Sure you might sound like a giant pussy, but at least you will get out of there.

➤ STEP #2: *Wait It Out*

Admit defeat. No one heard you. But sooner or later someone else will have to go to the bathroom and they'll let you out.

➤ STEP #3: *Take a Nap*

It's been hours and no one has come. Fuck it. Take advantage of the situation. This is not your fault; you're the victim here. Lay down and take a little nap. There's nothing better than taking an afternoon snooze where people go to shit.

Worst Places to Be Stuck

- Elevator

- Coffin

- Phone Booth

- Death Row

- Detroit

WTF: UP CLOSE AND PERSONAL

While visiting my wife's family in Brazil (yes, my wife is from Brazil and hot and you, by comparison, are a loser), I got locked in a gas station's bathroom, which was located outside and all the way in the back. Speaking little to no Portuguese, I yelled "gringo banero aqui!" which translates to "white jerk in the bathroom." For over five minutes, I pounded and screamed "gringo banero aqui!" over and over again. Covered in sweat (it was hot as balls outside) I panicked; my heart raced.

Finally, a policeman who happened to be at the gas station opened the door, laughing wildly. Then, he turned around and took a piss right there outside the gas station. Viva Brazil!

—GB

16. You Get Caught Wearing the Same Pants All Week

In college, wearing the same item of clothing until it was ripe enough that it could walk by itself was the norm. Everyone did it. Okay, maybe not *everyone*, but every scumbag that you hung out with, anyway. But now these squares you work with notice the little things in life, like you wearing the same smelly pants every day. WTF?

The WTF Approach to Looking the F*#!-ing Part

➤ OPTION #1: *Buy Some New Pants*

It's that easy. If you can't afford to buy new clothes then buy some clothing dye and color your pants every other day. Trendy!

➤ OPTION #2: *Steal Some Pants*

Go to the gym and work out around guys who look like the same size as you. Then when they go take a shower, take off with their pants.

➤ OPTION #3: *Own It*

If someone asks just say, "Yeah, these pants are very special to me. My father died in these pants and I never plan on taking them off." If your father is still alive just make sure no one ever meets him. That shouldn't be a problem.

Chances are, he disowned a loser like you years ago.

> **OPTION #4: *Flip the Switch***

If someone makes a comment about you wearing the same pants for over a week, accuse them of stalking you. Who keeps track of what other people wear? Report his ass to HR and tell them that is harassment and you plan to file a suit.

Matching Game

Match the outfit with corresponding profession:

1. Three piece suit
2. Khakis and polo shirt
3. Jeans and white, armpit-stained t-shirt
4. One glittery glove
5. Nothing

A. Security guard
B. Dead pop star
C. Trust fund baby
D. Mannequin after store closes
E. Construction worker

ANSWER KEY
1. A, **2.** C, **3.** E, **4.** B, **5.** D

17. Your Boss Catches You Falling Asleep at Your Desk

Maybe you were out partying, maybe you were just stressing out over life, or maybe you were "experimenting" with massive amounts of crack cocaine—whatever the reason, you're dead tired and you just can't stop dozing off at your desk. The next thing you know your boss is standing over you with that "you're about to get fired" look on his face. Think fast!

The WTF Approach to Getting Out of F*#!-ing Trouble

►OPTION #1: *Play Dumb*

Claim that this has never happened to you before and it might be a sudden case of narcolepsy. Tell him you should really leave work early and go to the doctor. Then go home and take a nice nap. When your boss asks what the doctor said, tell him it was just a case of low blood sugar.

►OPTION #2: *Start Crying*

Beg for his forgiveness and make up some bullshit story about a death in the family or your wife leaving you. Just keep crying, odds are he'll tell you to take the rest of the day off. Everyone will make fun of you behind your back, but fuck 'em. While they're busting your ass you'll be busting a nut—right before a big, fat nap.

► OPTION #3: *Flip the Switch*

Tell him you were sleeping because the work they expect you to do is so boring and tedious it would put anyone to sleep. Tell him you took this job expecting to be challenged only to find your potential being wasted. You might end up getting a promotion. Or fired.

IN THE FUTURE . . .

Learn how to sleep with your eyes open. Or better yet, wear sunglasses and say the florescent lights are hurting your eyes. Sure you'll look like a douche bag, but this way you can grab a quick nap without getting caught.

Best Places to Fall Asleep

* Between two massive breasts

* Between two gorgeous ass cheeks

* Between . . . [insert your particular sexual perversion here]

Worst Places to Fall Asleep

* On a tightrope

* Woods where they shot *Deliverance*

* On a bed of nails

18. You Have *Way* Too Many Bosses

"**D**id you get the memo?" "Did you get the memo?" "Did you get the memo?" "Did you get the . . ."

"Yes, I got the fucking memo!"

It's one thing to get an update from your boss—*one* boss. It's quite another thing to get the same update from a hundred bosses throughout the day. You're going insane and you can't take it anymore.

The WTF Approach to Dealing with a F*#!-ing Boss Parade

► **OPTION #1: *Become a Boss***

There are so many of them they might not even realize. Just start going around bothering people the way your "bosses" have pestered you for so long. If you can't beat 'em, join 'em.

► **OPTION #2: *Divide and Conquer***

Play these so-called bosses against one another. Spread rumors, send incriminating e-mails from their computers, and spill coffee on one of their desks with a note that reads: "Fuck you. [sign another boss's name]" Sit back and watch them destroy each other one by one. It's like a Shakespeare play, but less interesting.

➤ OPTION #3: *Embrace it*

This is your chance to shine . . . over and over and over again.

WTF Tip

Here are a few common phrases to get your bosses off your back . . .

- "I'm working on it, chief."

- "You'll have it by the end of the day"

- "Just putting the final touches on it."

- "You know me, I'm a perfectionist."

- "I got a hooker pregnant and I have to take her to the abortion clinic before my wife finds out."

for the ladies . . .

All you have to say is "I am bleeding profusely out of my vagina."

IN THE FUTURE . . .

Work for yourself. Then you only have one ass-hole to answer to.

Professions with Too Many Bosses

- Soldier

- Mafioso

- Plantation hand

19. Your Boss Keeps Calling You by the Wrong Name

It's been over a month since you started working and your boss still doesn't know your name. You feel like shouting out, "It's Greg, not Craig!" every time he calls for you. But there never seems to be the right moment to point it out and, considering your boss's quick temper, you don't want to push your luck. But enough is enough already. He should know who the hell you are by now. What to do, what to do . . .

The WTF Approach to Getting Some F*#!-ing Respect

► OPTION #1: *Wear a Name Tag*

"Hello my name is . . ." At first people may make fun of you, but tell them that you feel that wearing name tags makes the work environment friendlier—as if you are all part of the same team. Not only will wearing a name tag make the boss start calling you by your real name, he might promote you if the name-tag thing catches on. He might even call a special meeting to strongly encourage everyone to wear name tags. Don't worry, though, he'll give you credit for starting the trend. "Craig had a great idea when he started this name tag thing." FUCK!

➤ OPTION #2: *Suck It Up*

Don't push your luck. Let him call you "asshole" for all you care—just as long as you get a paycheck.

➤ OPTION #3: *Change Your Name*

Legally change your name to match whatever he is calling you. This way you can be referred to by your correct name without confronting him.

➤ OPTION #4: *Flip the Switch*

Call him by the wrong name and see how he likes it. Some good names are "Jerk face," "Bozo," "Shit-for-Brains" and, of course, "Cock sucking, piece of fucking shit, mother-fucking asshole."

What's in a Name?

Certain names go with certain kinds of people. Here is a breakdown of some names and the kind of worker they usually correspond to.

- Seth: Skinny and wiry, like a snake that thinks he's hot shit. He was the bad kid in school, the troublemaker. Watch out for him—he'll stab you in the back to get ahead.

- Jennifer: Hot blonde receptionist with upturned nose and bitchy adolescent voice who used to play volleyball but now plays with the boss's balls instead.

- Chad: Short, blond former high school soccer player who realizes now that his glory days are long over. He's average in every way, and knows it.

- Ira: Smart, but also a whiny little bitch.

- Doris: A sweetheart, but *way* too old to screw.

- Bobby Jo: She's a total redneck chick, but hot as hell. She loves shooting guns almost as much as sucking cock . . . almost. She's the party girl who, after downing a bottle of Jack, tried to blow Santa at the annual Christmas party . . . twice.

- Boris: A fat Russian pig.

- Jodi: Hot, funny, lonely— probably has a cat but is still out of your league.

- Greg: Good-looking, funny, life of the party, good-looking, wonderful, good-looking . . . did we mention he is attractive?

20. Everyone Keeps Passing Their Work on to You

"Hey, buddy. How's it going? When you get a chance take a look at this would you? Thanks, pal." And that's it. You're now stuck doing someone else's work. While one or two extra assignments would be okay, ever since you started the job it seems like everyone is pushing off their work on you. It's too much. You just can't do it anymore. But you're the new guy and you don't want to make waves. WTF?

The WTF Approach to Dealing with the F*#!-ing Workflow

➤ OPTION #1: *Just Do It*

Suck it up and do everything everyone asks of you. You know that you're weak, so don't fight it. Embrace that weakness and convince yourself it's really a matter of being kind and helping others.

➤ OPTION #2: *Do Their Work Poorly*

Make sure your assignments shine, while theirs suck. As long as you do your job and please your supervisor, you should be fine. Your peers will think you're a moron, but it's better than being a slave.

➤ OPTION #3: *Just Say No*

You were hired to do a specific job, not as a random errand boy. Tell them you are swamped and that you can't do it. Make sure to tell them you have spoken to your superior and they agreed that you should focus on your own work.

➤ OPTION #4: *Make a Trade*

When someone gives you work, take it and thank them. Then hand them work of your own. Before they can speak, say "good trade" and walk away.

➤ OPTION #5: *Write a Stirring Mission Statement*

Be like Jerry Maguire and write a heart-wrenching mission statement about everyone doing their part to help the company. Make sure you take the goldfish and the overrated squinty mousey chick with you when you get canned. Don't worry; you'll love her little boy with the freakishly large head.

ARE PEOPLE TAKING ADVANTAGE OF YOU?

You might be doing more than your job description. A quick checklist to see if you're becoming the office lackey:

❏ The receptionist asks you to do her toenails.

❏ The mailroom asks for your help licking envelopes.

❏ The intern convinced you that running coffee was your responsibility, not hers.

❏ You get excited about the weekend because finally you can catch up on your work.

❏ Your boss asks you to squeeze his balls while he bangs his secretary.

21. No One Will Speak to You

It's been three weeks since you started and not a friggin' peep. No one will give you the time of day—even when you literally ask for the time of day. You like your work, but this is the loneliest job in history. Day after day, not even a glance from a coworker. And forget about Fridays; they're the worst. When everyone is going out for happy hour, you're going home in traffic, with only your tears to keep you company.

The WTF Approach to Being F*#!-ing Noticed

> **STEP #1: Get a Kleenex**

Stop crying and act like a god-damn man for once!

> **STEP #2: Change Your Appearance**

Whatever look you are going for obviously isn't working. Get a haircut and a new wardrobe—particularly something flashy or outrageous. This should get you some attention and may work as a conversation starter.

> **STEP #3: Ride a Motorcycle**

Motorcycles are cool, and every-one likes to talk about them. Trade in your Prius for a Harley and make believe you are too cool for school. Don't, however, use that expression, which is a dead give-away that you are not too cool for anything.

➤ STEP #4: *Learn the Art of Sword-swallowing*

Or juggling. Or knife throwing. Or anything that can make you stand out during company meetings. Surely that's got to get someone talking.

➤ STEP #5: *Get Really Sick*

If you get really, really sick—like to the point where you almost die—people will be forced to talk to you when you recover, at least to welcome you back. Ideally, you should get sick while you are at work so everyone can see you leave in an ambulance. This will guarantee enough sympathy points to open up some sort of dialogue.

➤ STEP #6: *Jerk Off*

Fuck it. Apparently no one is paying attention to you anyhow, you might as well enjoy yourself.

GREAT MASTURBATION QUOTES

"We have reason to believe that man first walked upright to free his hands for masturbation."—Lily Tomlin

"Intercourse with a woman is sometimes a satisfactory substitute for masturbation. But it takes a lot of imagination to make it work."—Karl Kraus

"Don't knock masturbation; it's sex with someone I love."—Woody Allen

"Philosophy is to the real world what masturbation is to sex."—Karl Marx

"The good thing about masturbation is that you don't have to dress up for it."—Truman Capote

Smile and the World Smiles with You

Laughing and smiling are important. Acting like you are having a good time makes people want to talk to you—especially girls. Always have a smile on your face, even if you have good reason to hate yourself and your life. If you have a hard time smiling on cue, think about some of your favorite things like raindrops on roses, whiskers on kittens, bright copper kettles, and a warm pussy hole.

Jobs That Don't Require Talking

- Professional golfer
- Meter maid
- Tollbooth operator
- Silent movie actor

IN THE FUTURE . . .

Become a mime. Everyone loves a mime. Paint your face white, get a crazy outfit, and find a street corner. Start performing for cash and you never have to speak to anyone again.

22. You Don't Know When to Leave

There's a learning curve to everything at a new job, even when it comes to knowing when you can get the hell out of there on a Friday. Understanding when the workday is officially over can be a tricky thing if you don't have a job where you punch a clock. So there you are, it's five o'clock and you don't know if you can leave—and you don't want to rock the boat. What to do?

The WTF Approach to Leaving the F*#!-ing Office

➤ **OPTION #1:** *Leave.*

➤ **OPTION #2:** *Don't leave.*

You need a fucking book to figure this out, jackass?

Just Kidding . . .

Don't get your panties in a bunch. This *is* a difficult situation to navigate, and we're going to help.

➤ OPTION #3: *Ask Around*

Check with a few of your coworkers and find out what the bosses expect. Best to find someone who has worked under your particular supervisor and can give you the real scoop.

➤ OPTION #4: *Leave Early*

Be one of the first people to leave the office every day. The worst case scenario is that your boss confronts you and tells you to stay later. Make sure all your work is complete so you can claim you were done for the day as an excuse. This is much better than setting the precedent of you leaving late. Most bosses only notice when you are inconsistent. Come late and leave early until they confront you.

Are You Working Too Late?

- When you leave your 9-to-5 job, you hit rush hour—morning rush hour.

- Your girlfriend/wife is certain that you are cheating on her during these "late work nights."

- The last time you slept a full eight hours was that week you spent in a coma after a horrendous bicycle accident.

- Your idea of a vacation is reading *Travel* magazine in the bathroom at lunch.

- You started working in late spring 2007—and you left five minutes ago.

23. You Don't Know How to Use the Copier

Load paper. Load paper. Load paper. What? But you just did load paper! It's there and you can see it with your own eyes! What the f*#! is this goddamn machine's problem? How come it works just fine when anyone else uses it? You have a college degree for God's sake. Is this devil machine out to get you? Or are you completely inept?

Yes to both answers, dipshit.

The WTF Approach to Dealing with a Demonic F*#!-ing Copier

➤ STEP #1: *Get Help*

Make sure to ask someone lower than you on the food chain—you don't want your peers or superiors to know you're incapable of doing something as simple as making copies. If you are the lowest on the food chain, your job is probably heavily dependent on mak-ing copies. Move on to Step #2 or start looking for new employment ASAP.

➤ STEP #2: *Strike a Deal with It*

You know, the way you do when your car doesn't start. Tell the copy machine that you will be forever indebted to it if it works for you—just this once! Then feel silly about trying to negotiate with an inanimate object.

➤ STEP #3: *Use Positive Thought*

See it happening, and then make it a reality. Visualize the copy successfully going through, and then put that idea into the world. Read *The Secret* if you need further assistance, jerk off.

➤ STEP #4: *Destroy It*

When that bullshit doesn't work, show it who's boss. Who can forget the scene in *Office Space* where the three main characters take a baseball bat to the printer in a deserted field? Rape that friggin' thing until it squeals.

> **NOTE:** Raping office equipment is legal. Raping office personnel is not. Remember that.

for the ladies . . .

Just ask a man. Men are always willing to help a woman. You may have to sleep with them as a form of gratitude. No pain, no gain.

Also Difficult to Operate . . .

- Soundboards
- Bulldozers
- Vaginas

24. You Get Caught Making Personal Calls

You try and fake it like you are speaking to a client: "Um, okay. Right. Well, that sounds good then. Okay, well have a great day and we'll talk soon. I love you."

We said you *try*, but you don't get away with it. It seems like every time you make a personal call your boss just happens to pass by. And guess what, he doesn't care whether or not leftover spaghetti for dinner is okay with you.

The WTF Approach to Taking Personal F*#!-ing Calls

➤ OPTION #1: *Talk More Quietly*

Maybe you just have a loud voice that carries? Tone it down a notch and maybe no one will overhear your calls. However, make sure to maintain a consistent level of volume on all calls, business-related as well as personal. You don't want to arouse any suspicion when you're overheard speaking quietly.

➤ OPTION #2: *Stick to Yes or No Answers*

If your girlfriend calls you and asks if you want your balls drained after work, just say "yes" or "no" depending how you feel. Don't say "Yes, I would love to have my balls drained." Pretend you're being cross-examined on the stand and she's a really, really horny attorney.

➤ OPTION #3: *Make Up a Code*

Develop a code that you can use with your friends and girlfriend. Examples:

WHAT YOU SAY	WHAT YOU MEAN
I'm going to need that spread sheet.	Spread a clean sheet down on the bed before I get home, bitch.
You are my favorite client.	I love the way you look naked.
The numbers don't line up.	Let's order out. No, not Chinese. What about that little Thai place around the corner? Yeah, that one.

WHAT THE F*#! IS UP WITH . . .

NOT BEING ABLE TO HANDLE PERSONAL SHIT AT WORK

If you work from 9 to 5, five days a week with a shitty half-hour lunch break which most of the time you spend at your desk because you are swamped, then when the fuck are you supposed to handle all the personal shit you need to if not at work? The annoying details of contemporary life require an exorbitant amount of time. Talking to your insurance carrier, your bank, or God forbid the DMV requires hours of time. Bosses must understand that their employees have lives outside of their shitty jobs. So let them make a couple phone calls at work because you goddamn well know that's the only time they can.

for the ladies . . .

Just give the boss that "Oh no you didn't!" look when he complains about your personal calls.

chapter three

making your mark

25. Your Coworker Takes Credit for Your Work

You worked long and hard on this important account and now you are ready to reap the rewards. This is probably your best work. Surely you'll get noticed now. But when you strut into your boss's office to show off the product of your labor you find your coworker's already there—presenting it as if it were his own!

The WTF Approach to Getting F*#!-ing Credit

➤ OPTION #1: *Tattle*

Tell your boss straight up that this asshole stole your work. You'll look like a big old cry baby but screw it, you did the work and you deserve the credit. If the coworker puts up a fight, beat the living shit out of him until he passes out in a pool of his own rotten blood.

➤ OPTION #2: *Challenge Him*

In front of your boss, congratulate him on a job well done, and then ask him how he came up with all of these amazing ideas. What inspired him? Then sit back and watch the pig sweat.

➤ OPTION #3: *Kidnap His Little Girl*

Stealing is stealing. Two can play at that game.

➤ OPTION #4: *Do Nothing*

Crawl back to your desk with your little tiny balls between your legs like the pathetic dog that you are.

Work Is No Laughing Matter

"The world is divided into people who do things—and people who get the credit."

—DWIGHT MORROW

Princes and Princesses of Thieves

Famous people who are accused of stealing others hard work

- Elizabeth Hasselbeck: Sued by another author who accused her of stealing ideas for her book *The G Free Diet: A Gluten-Free Survival Guide*.

- Poincaré: His ideas weren't publicly available when Einstein supposedly stole them.

- Milton Berle: Constantly accused of stealing jokes.

- Alexander Graham Bell: Allegedly took undeserved credit for the telephone.

- Helen Keller: She stole the spotlight from hardworking little girls who could see, hear, and speak. Selfish bitch!

26. Your Assistant Is After Your Job

At first, he seemed like the perfect assistant. He did everything you asked him to and more, going above and beyond the call of duty. He was ambitious, hardworking, and even reminded you of yourself when you were fifteen pounds lighter and still had dreams. But then you notice that he might be a little *too* ambitious, and not have your best interest at heart. He starts palling around with *your* boss, taking on assignments from other partners, and leaving work whenever he feels like it. Then you hear the unthinkable from a trusted colleague: This little prick is making a play for *your* job.

The WTF Approach to Keeping Him F*#!-ing Down

➤ STEP #1: *Threaten Him*

Call him into your office and talk to him man to man—or rather man to little conniving prick. Tell him that you know what he is doing and that if he doesn't stop you will make his life a living hell. Mention your time in Vietnam or Iraq, even if you never served and are a complete coward.

➤ STEP #2: *Embarrass Him*

If he doesn't take your threat seriously, bring him into a meeting with the partners and then ask him to go get coffee and doughnuts for everyone. Make fun of him behind his back so when he returns everyone can't help but laugh at his expense.

➤ STEP #3: *Make Him Everyone's Enemy*

Burn his bridges. Send a nasty e-mail from his computer filled with derogatory comments about everyone in the office including the boss and CC all your other coworkers. Then we'll see how popular he is.

➤ STEP #4: *Get Him Fired*

He still hasn't wised up? Here are some creative ways to get him the boot:

- Put a banana in the exhaust pipe of his car and destroy his transmission before a critical early morning meeting.

- Take the CEO's family picture off his desk, ejaculate on it, and leave it in your assistant's cubicle.

- Pay a pregnant street hooker to come into the office and demand that he accept his love child.

- Leave a couple pieces of paper with swastikas doodled on them on his desk.

ALWAYS REMEMBER ...

Never socialize. He's your bitch, not your buddy.

IN THE FUTURE . . .

Save yourself the trouble and just have him transferred. Make the case that your ambitious little self-starter would be even more useful to the satellite office in Anchorage.

27. You Get Turned Down for a Much Deserved Raise

There is nothing worse than not being acknowledged for a job well done. And for the last several months you have been busting your ass. Coming in early, staying late, and basically giving up on any chance at a social life. So when it's time for your review you're confident that you'll get a glowing report and a raise to go with it. But you only get the praise, not the raise. WTF?!

The WTF Approach to Getting F*#!-ing Paid

➤ OPTION #1: *Stand Tall*

Come from a position of strength. Explain to your boss that you've earned that raise and that you are extremely disappointed your work is not being appreciated. Hint that you've received better offers from other companies. Careful though, he might tell you to take them. Then you're totally screwed.

➤ OPTION #2: *Stand Short*

Invent a sob story and beg like a dog. You were counting on the raise to pay for a new liver for your wife who is dying of a terrible condition called liver, you know, um . . . well, liver *something* anyway.

➤ OPTION #3: *Slack Off*

If you're not getting a raise, fuck praise. Stop putting in all that time and energy. Just do enough to get by as you look for another gig.

MY DYING WIFE

➤ OPTION #4: *Shut Up and Take It*

Kids are starving in Newark. Be happy you have a job at all you inconsiderate piece of shit!

for the ladies . . .

Drop your pants and earn that promotion the old fashion way.

HEADHUNTER'S TIP

There's a right way and wrong way to ask for a raise.

Right Way: I believe that I have shown to be a critical asset to the company, proving time and time again that I can excel in any situation, and accomplish any task handed to me. Recently, as I have taken on additional work and responsibilities, I believe that I have earned and should receive a pay raise commensurate with these new duties.

Wrong Way: I need money or these guys are going to kill me!

28. You Get Demoted

You have worked at your job for years and done everything that's asked of you. You know things are tight, so you aren't expecting a raise this year. But when you get called into your boss's office and told that you are getting demoted, you feel like you've been kicked in the balls.

The WTF Approach to Handling the Bad F*#!-ing News

➤ OPTION #1: *Quit*

If you really can't handle the shame then quit and go look for a job that pays you what you deserve.

➤ OPTION #2: *Say Thank You*

You need to be grateful that you weren't let go all together you ungrateful fucknut! And if you were demoted for not doing your job as well as you could, then get your shit together . . . duh!

World's Worst Demotions

	PREVIOUS POSITION	AFTER DEMOTION
Napoleon	Emperor of the French, King of Italy, Ruler of Europe	Prisoner on the island of St. Helena; reduced to begging for "freedom" fries
Julius Caesar	Roman Emperor	High-calorie salad
Abraham Lincoln	President of the United States	Dead
The United States	World's only Superpower	Broke shit-hole owned by the Chinese

World's Best Promotions

	PREVIOUS POSITION	AFTER DEMOTION
Sarah Palin	Brainless beauty queen	Vice presidential candidate and major political force
Barack Obama	Unknown congressman with a nice smile and good grammar	President of the United States
China	Overpopulated shit-hole with no money, food, or significance	Overpopulated shit-hole with a ton of cash and U.S. treasury bonds

29. You're Being Transferred to Alaska

When your boss told you that you were being transferred, you could barely hide your excitement. Maybe
you'll get to go to the New York office? Or the Los Angeles
office? Or the new office in Las Vegas? The idea of taking a
stroll down Central Park in the fall, sitting on a beach watching hot blondes in bikinis roller skating, or blowing all your
savings on blackjack and hookers sounds like a hell of a lot
more fun than drinking draft beer at your local hotspot in
your current city of Shitsville, USA. But then the boss tells you
where you're going: Alaska. Yes, fucking Alaska!

The WTF Approach to Dealing with the F*#!-ing Relocation

➤ **OPTION #1:** *Go*

Hey, it could be an adventure—
and not just the kind of outdoor
hiking one you're thinking of. The
capital, Anchorage, has one of
the highest per capita prostitute
populations in the world.

WTFACT: Men out-number women almost
10 to 1 in the state.

➤ **OPTION #2:** *Take a Stand*

Tell the boss that you cannot and
will not go under any circumstances. Lie and say that you have

an illness that makes you unable
to withstand the cold. Or tell him
that you have such a little dick
that the shrinkage factor in the
arctic will be just too intolerable
and embarrassing. He'll probably
sympathize with you and let you
stay. But be prepared to overhear
the girls giggling at you in the
office the next day because you
know that he's going to talk.

ALASKAN INDEPENDENCE?

Forget about the South rising again,
the Alaskan Independence Party—a
major political party in the state—has
been advocating succession for
decades. How serious are they? Joe
Volger, the founder of the Party, stated
in an interview that the "fires of hell
are frozen glaciers compared to my
hatred for the American government."
And that he "won't be buried under
their damn flag."

Top Five Reasons Why Alaskans Wants to Secede

1. Embarrassment over the "Bridge to Nowhere"

2. Anger over Americans constantly forgetting it's a state

3. Want to make Inuit official language

4. Want to legalize and encourage polar bear fucking/killing

5. Shitload of oil at their disposal

Top Five Reasons Why America Wants to Keep Alaska

1. With Alaska, get to brag that the country is bigger than China

2. Cheaper tax on import of Russian mail order brides

3. The term "Eskimo-American" is just too funny

4. *Northern Exposure* was a great show

5. Shitload of oil at their disposal

STUFF ESKIMOS LIKE

You may have heard of the bestseller *Stuff White People Like,* well following is a list of things Eskimos like from the less popular book, *Stuff Eskimos Like*:

- Ice

- Snow

- Sleet

- Water vapor

- Being fucking dwarves

---

30. You Pass Gas During a Pivotal Presentation

You've prepared all week for this friggin' thing, practicing in front of the mirror countless times. Finally, the day has come for you to shine, the day where you finally get the respect and the promotion you've been working toward for so long. You're not nervous, you're as solid as a rock, and everything is going as smoothly as possible. Your ideas are clear; your delivery is confident; you've got the whole boardroom in the palm of your hand. Then, just when things couldn't get better, you let out the biggest goddamn disgusting wet sloppy fart of your entire life. Fuck!

The WTF Approach to Covering Up Your Stinky F*#!-ing Fart

➤ **OPTION #1: _Pretend Nothing Happened_**

Keep going, and focus your eyes on a picture in the back of the room. Do not look these people in the eye. Stand tall and finish your presentation—squeezing your ass checks to prevent another slip. Who knows, maybe they'll be so captivated with your sales projections that they'll forget how disgusting you are.

➤ OPTION #2: *Laugh It Off*

Let out a laugh and look at everyone in the room. Connect with them. Everyone has farted before, so who the fuck are they to judge?

➤ OPTION #3: *Incorporate It*

Make the fart part of the presentation. Say that consumers are going to be so happy about the new widget that they'll fart or shit their pants. They'll be thankful that, as a show of good taste, you refrained from demonstrating the latter.

➤ OPTION #4: *Walk Out*

Do you really want to see these people again? It's over. You'll be a laughing stock forever. Walk out and let another one rip on your way to the door.

***WTF*FACT:** You are the only person disgusting enough to ever do this. You fucking freak!

HEADHUNTER'S TIP

Do not mention this event as a funny anecdote at your next big interview.

Different Kinds of Farts

Shart: A more polite way of saying you just shit your pants like a pig.

Silent killer: These farts make no noise, but rate a 10 on the stink scale. Remember the maxim that "whoever smelt it, dealt it." If you can't control your asshole, at least keep your mouth shut so you don't get blamed.

Whoopee cushion fart: This kind is loud and resembles the type of sound that a whoopee cushion makes. It might not stink, but it's impossible to hide the fact that you were indeed the farter.

Little dumb kid fart: It's the type let out by stupid little kids that laugh and think it's funny because they have yet to learn how to live in polite society.

Death fart: This fart is so powerful that it pushes all your internal organs outside of your asshole. Seriously, keep regular and eat your grapes so you don't end up dying this way.

WHEN YOU *SHOULDN'T* FART

- On an airplane
- While fighting fire in a burning building
- In a patrol car for a minor violation
- During confession
- While you're getting a blow job
- While giving a blow job

WHEN YOU *SHOULD* FART

- Bosses office on your way out. Best to make sure it's silent, but violent
- In a bathroom
- In the cashier's line—it's bound to speed things up
- The empty elevator before you get off
- Your coworker's cubicle
- When you're deep sea diving
- In your car if you've been carjacked

31. You Have a Bad Case of Carpal Tunnel Syndrome

It was bound to happen. After years of toiling away in corporate America you are finally stricken by the Yuppie's most feared malady: the dreaded carpal tunnel syndrome. Now, with work piling up on your desk, you can't seem to type a letter without wincing in pain, holding your hand like a bitch.

The WTF Approach to Fixing Your F*#!-ing Hands

➤ **OPTION #1: *Rub It Out***

Go to an Asian massage parlor and get a hand massage. In fact, it doesn't even have to be an Asian masseuse as long as the person is small, wiry, and has high cheekbones.

➤ **OPTION #2: *Ice It***

Everyone says to just "put some ice on it" when you're in pain. Of course, it doesn't really do shit, but do it anyway since that's what every asshole suggests.

➤ **OPTION #3: *Be Like Stephen Hawking***

Get a fancy voice synthesizer like the famous scientist, Stephen Hawking. If he can uncover the mysteries of the universe without typing, you can figure out how to finish your next mindless "project."

➤ OPTION #4: *Get a Cheap Secretary*

Hire some recently homeless college graduate to type up your shit for gas money and a few beers.

➤ OPTION #5: *Shut the Fuck Up*

Stop whining and be lucky that you have hands, let alone a job. Do you know how many young children become armless and legless every year in Cambodia and other war torn nations riddled with minefields? How can you be so fucking selfish and insensitive?

Other Bullshit Sounding Syndromes

- **Bra-strap headache syndrome:** Chronic pain in the back of the neck muscles that radiates to the top of the head. A result of a tight-fitting bra. Usually happens to women with *huge* tits.

- **Traumatic Masturbatory Syndrome:** This *weird* syndrome is a result of years of masturbation where your thrusts are controlled by hand grip and that makes it harder for you to carry on with the same rhythm and strength during actual sex. Sufferers usually lack sensitivity in their sexual organs and finally succumb to desensitization.

NOTE: Stop yanking it asshole!

- **Baddiel's Syndrome:** Fear of animatronic toys (vibrators in particular)

- **Syndrome Syndrome:** All modern doctors have been showing symptoms of this syndrome. It's where they can't stop making up syndromes and disorders to diagnose people with.

chapter four

office
politics

32. You Get Accused of Sexual Harassment

All you said was "nice shirt" and now everyone is treating you differently. The stares, the whispers, the evil looks. Then you get called into HR to find your boss, a lawyer, and that woman you complimented. Yep, you're getting accused of sexual harassment. WTF?

The WTF Approach to Being Really F*#!-ing Screwed

➤ STEP #1: *Deny It*

Unless they have proof, deny it until you die. If they keep it up, sue their asses for slander and cash in.

➤ STEP #2: *Bring Her Flowers*

Smooth things over with your accuser even if you didn't do anything, and even if she is a fucking bitch. Bring her flowers and all will be good. Flowers are a rem-edy for anything you do wrong with a woman. You can forget her birthday, cheat on her, even tell her how fat her ass is— once she opens the door to see you with a dozen roses all is forgiven.

➤ STEP #3: *Start Harassing Everyone*

Better not let this happen again. If you are getting accused of treating a particular person a particular way, start treating everyone the same way. Grab asses, send perverted e-mails, and add "in bed" to anything you say. Example: "Can you with help me on this project . . . in bed?" Then sit back and watch the fireworks.

> **NOTE:** We are not responsible in any way if you do decide to sexually harass your coworkers. But we do envy how much fun you'll have.

What Not *to Do*

Yell out: "You know you want me bitch!"

for the ladies . . .

Even if you aren't guilty, let them fire you. Whatever you get sued for won't be close to the kind of money you'll make when you sell the rights of this sexy story to *Lifetime*. Everyone loves the idea of a female sexual harasser.

WTF ABOUT TOWN

We here at *WTF* have your best interest in mind. So we've decided to help you navigate that fine line between sexual harassment and harmless flirtation.

SEXUAL HARASSMENT

WTF: Wow, you look very nice today.

Employee: Thank you.

WTF: Show me your tits!

HARMLESS FLIRTATION

WTF: Wow, you look very nice today.

Employee: Thank you.

WTF: May I *please* see your tits?

33. You're Getting Sexually Harassed

You never thought you'd be in this position. With only three Winks in the last year on Match.com, you can barely get a date, let alone entice a woman so much that she harasses you. But sexual harassment is about power, not about sex. At first your female boss just flirted with you occasionally—a little wink here and a little pat on the lower back there. But one day she calls you into her office, closes the blinds, and grabs your package. "Fuck me," she says. "Right now!"

The WTF Approach to Getting F*#!-ing Molested

➤ OPTION #1: *Just Go with It*

Duh! Give the old bag what she needs. Close your eyes and picture the hot blonde college intern in the Marketing Department you could never get and bang the old broad into next week.

➤ OPTION #2: *Get Help*

Run out and call a lawyer. Sue the shit out of her and the company. Make sure you get tons of publicity. Write a book that gets turned into a movie so you never have to work another friggin' job again.

➤ OPTION #3: *Blackmail*

Just threaten to sue her and use that as leverage. Ask for a better office, a raise, and more vacation time.

WHAT THE F*#! IS UP WITH . . .
POLITICIANS BEING SUCH WHORES

Senators, governors, and even U.S. presidents seem to be getting caught left and right in extramarital activities. But why all the shock and uproar? Sure these respected government figures run states and nations, but the fact is they have dicks, and their dicks run *them*.

---

for the ladies . . .

Sue. In fact, even if you are not sexually harassed sue anyway. Play the victim and they'll settle without a fight.

Work Is No Laughing Matter

"When a man talks dirty to a woman, its sexual harassment. When a woman talks dirty to a man, it's $3.95 a minute."

—ANONYMOUS

Sexual Harassment May Be . . .

❏ Unwanted sexual advances

❏ Requests for sexual favors

❏ Inappropriate jokes

❏ Finding naked pictures of you on the office computers

❏ Trying to blow yourself at your desk

34. Your Boss Takes You to a Strip Club

It's the right of passage for someone working their way up the corporate ladder. The boss starts asking you to join him for lunch, then for a round of golf, then maybe even over to his house for Sunday dinner. But when your boss decides to take you to a strip club, you're not sure how to react.

The WTF Approach to Seeing Strippers with the F*#!-ing Boss Man

➤ OPTION #1: *Go!*

Duh? Why wouldn't you? It's not like he's asking you to go with him for a colonoscopy for God's sake. Grow some balls and get a lap dance, pussy. Be sure to take a photo with your iPhone of your boss getting one too. Great for future blackmail!

➤ OPTION #2: *Tell Him You're Gay*

Confess to him that you like dudes. Sure, now you might have to endure all the talk behind your back about being gay, but at least this guarantees your job security. He can't fire you now. That would be discriminatory. Fat lawsuit!

➤ **OPTION #3:** *Politely Decline*

Tell him you really need to stay and get your work done. Also your girlfriend/wife would have your balls if she found out.

Top Ten Female Stripper Names

Here's a list according to *Bacon Magazine:*

1. Destiny
2. Candy
3. Angel
4. Cherry
5. Raven
6. Anastasia
7. Roxy
8. Houston
9. Porsche
10. Crystal

TOP FIVE MALE STRIPPER NAMES

Here's a list according to *WTF:*

1. Billy Blue Balls
2. Sammy Six-pack
3. Gary "Big Guns"
4. Mr. Cock
5. Abraham

Work Is No Laughing Matter

"If you think your boss is stupid, remember: you wouldn't have a job if he was any smarter."

—JOHN GOTTI

for the ladies . . .

Hot—no matter how you look at it!

35. Your Boss Hits on Your Girl

At first you dismissed his flirtations. You figured that he calls every girl "sweetheart," so it should be no different when your girl comes in to see you at the office. And so what if it looks like he stares at her ass once in a while? He does that with every chick. But when he touched her on the back and whispered in her ear that she "looked wonderful today," you knew you had to man up and do something about it. But what?

The WTF Approach to Dealing with a Horny F*#!-ing Boss

➤ OPTION #1: *Confront Him*

Be a man and tell him you won't take that shit from anyone, no matter how many diplomas they have on the wall of their office. Demand respect and you'll get it. Start looking for another job just in case.

➤ OPTION #2: *Use It*

Play this to your advantage. Accuse her of being receptive to his advances and then drop her like you've wanted to do for a few months now.

➤ **OPTION #3:** *Pimp Her Out*

Convince your girlfriend that banging your boss would be a good way for you to get a promotion. If she does it, take the promotion and then dump her for being a whore. Only God can save her now.

➤ **OPTION #4:** *Flip the Switch*

Hit on his girlfriend/wife. Screw her if she lets you and then tell him about it. If he's single, have sex with his mom.

Being Nice vs. Flirting

Sometimes it's hard to distinguish flirting from just being nice and gentlemanly. Here are some examples of this very fine line.

Being Nice: Asking what she did last weekend
Flirting: Asking who she did last weekend

Being Nice: Saying, "Hey, nice pants."
Flirting: Saying, "Hey, nice camel toe."

Being Nice: Laughing and smiling at everything she says
Flirting: Laughing and smiling at everything she says with your cock hanging out of your suit.

Being Nice: Opening the door for her
Flirting: Opening her vagina

NOTE: Some of the above might be even more than flirting, and may actually constitute sexual harassment. So before you pry open your coworker's vagina, check with Legal.

36. You Get Caught Stealing Office Supplies

It starts out innocently enough. Couple of envelopes here, some Scotch tape there, maybe a box of pens. Then before you know it you're leaving the office with a chair, a desk, and the vending machine strapped to your back. Your closet at home looks like an aisle at Office Max and now you can't stop, until the day a coworker catches you red-handed.

The WTF Approach to Being Caught Red F*#!-ing Handed

➤ STEP #1: *Lie*

Tell your coworker you are donating all of these office supplies to a needy charity. The children in Rwanda desperately need staplers. You are a philanthropist and you should be rewarded, not punished.

➤ STEP #2: *Bribe Her*

If she doesn't buy your BS, offer her a Hershey bar from the vending machine to keep her mouth shut. Every chick likes chocolate.

➤ STEP #3: *Flip the Switch*

Tell her that you are working on a top-secret assignment and the boss knows about it. Make sure to tell the busybody that if she gets involved it could cost her a job. Then immediately report her to HR and accuse her of stealing. Make sure to plant the vending machine in her purse.

WTFACT: The most common things "lost" in the office:

- Pens and pencils
- Paper
- Post-its
- Calculators
- Staplers
- Hopes, dreams, and the like

Water Cooler Talk

"Office supplies are like a buffet. You take all you can because it is there for you."

—Janet Fields, receptionist/moron

What's in a Name?

Why is it that everyone feels the need to change his title to sound more important?

BEFORE	AFTER
Secretary	Administrative assistant
Stewardess	Flight attendant
Friendly uncle	Pedophile

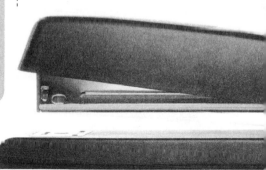

37. Someone Keeps Taking Your Stapler

It happens just about every day and always when you need it the most. You have a stack of papers on your desk that need stapling but when you reach over to get your stapler it's gone. Fucking scumbags.

The WTF Approach to Keeping People's Hands Off Your F*#!-ing Shit

> **OPTION #1: *Steal Someone Else's***

Make it some other chump's problem, just like you do with everything else in your life. Fair is fair, right? Well, not "fair" since the person you steal from didn't take your stapler, but there's no need to split hairs here. You have been wronged, so wrong someone else. Chaos or random chance is the only truly just and unprejudiced force in the world. Be its agent.

> **OPTION #2: *Steal Everyone's***

Take all the staplers in the office and hide them in the basement. Who's laughing now?

> **OPTION #3: *Smell Out the Thief***

Set up a web cam and catch that asshole red-handed. Then staple his hands together. Drastic maybe, but trust us, he will never steal anything again—or hold anything for that matter.

➤ OPTION #4: *Set Up a Booby Trap*

Rig small explosives to the stapler and blow the thief sky high, killing him instantly. When the boss complains that you've murdered a coworker, just explain that stealing is wrong, and God was watching.

➤ OPTION #5: *Set the Building on Fire*

Like the guy in *Office Space,* set the building ablaze and move to an island paradise. Make sure to grab a ton of cash (and staplers) before you light the flame.

> ### Work Is No Laughing Matter
>
> "Every day I get up and look through the *Forbes* list of the richest people in America. If I'm not there, I go to work."
>
> —ROBERT ORBEN

IN THE FUTURE . . .

Glue it down to your desk. Hotels nail down the remote and lamps, so why not do it with your stapler? If your boss tells you to un-glue it, steal his stapler and see how he likes it.

38. You Get Caught Eating Someone Else's Food

It's lunch time and, as usual, you're famished. Hurriedly, you reach in for your sandwich, take a bite, and discover something odd: for some reason, it doesn't taste like shit. In fact, you might even call it "good." You glance down at the wrapper and see your coworker's name on it. Shit! That's right, accidental though it may have been, you are now the office scumbag that steals people's food. How does it feel to be a fucking pig, pig?

The WTF Approach to Being a F*#!-ing Pig

➤ OPTION #1: *Put It Back*

A half-eaten gourmet sandwich is better than the whole one you made. He should share the wealth. Remember what Karl Marx said about the equal distribution of sandwiches? No? Well, he was all for it.

➤ OPTION #2: *Get Rid of the Evidence*

Finish it up quickly and shred the wrapper. No proof, no case. If he really wants some evidence he'll have to wait at least twenty-four hours until you crap it out.

> **OPTION #3: *Take Him to Lunch***

Offer to take the coworker out to lunch somewhere nice. Then take his spoiled gourmet ass to McDonald's so he can see how the other half lives.

> **OPTION #4: *Replace It***

Put something better in its place. Like a hooker. A really small one.

> **OPTION #5: *Blame It on Someone Else***

Pick someone that you really hate and blame it on her. Lie and say the same thing happened to you, and you're not going to take it anymore. People are less likely to question someone who seems outraged.

WTF ABOUT TOWN

We went to offices around town during lunch and staked out the refrigerators. It wasn't long before we witnessed a man eating someone else's sandwich. After being caught red-handed by the rightful owner, the following conversations ensued:

Sandwich Owner: Hey, is that my sandwich you're eating?

Thief: Wow, I guess it is. How about that? Did you bring a drink? I'm thirsty.

Water Cooler Talk

"Someone was always taking my food, no matter how many labels I put on it. Once I baked a special batch of chocolate chip cookies laced with laxatives, put them in a strategically placed Ziploc container, and watched the guilty party make frequent trips to the bathroom. Then I sent him an e-mail that said: 'Having a shitty day? You deserve it asshat!'"

—JC McBride, associate sales rep

39. Your Boss Eats Your Food

You do all the right things—you put a label on your lunch with your name on it; hide it in the fridge; retrieve it before the noon-time rush. But then one day you get called into your boss's office to find him chomping down on your food with no remorse. When you tell him it's yours he just winks and says, "Thanks. Now get back to work."

The WTF Approach to Losing Your F*#!-ing Lunch

➤ OPTION #1: *Beat the Shit Out of Him*

Then blame it on low blood sugar. You have to eat every three hours or else you blackout and do violent things. Sorry, but if he didn't eat your food this never would have happened.

➤ OPTION #2: *Appeal to His Gentler Side*

Explain to him, in great detail, the painstaking efforts your wife takes to make these sandwiches for you and how, considering you guys never sleep together anymore, this is the one thing that you share. He will feel so sorry for you, he might even buy *you* lunch—and get you a hooker to boot.

➤ OPTION #3: *Act Horrified*

Cover your mouth and gasp. When he asks what's wrong just tell him that "You might want to see a doctor immediately." Then turn around and go back to your desk. He'll be in the bathroom shoving his finger down his throat in no time. He'll never touch your food again.

HEADHUNTER'S TIP

Here are some foolproof labels that will ensure no one touches your sandwich:

CAUTION: HUMAN FECES SAMPLE

I MADE THIS WITH MY FEET

ROAD KILL ON RYE

VEGAN CHEESEBURGER

I HAVE HERPES . . .
AND SO DOES THIS SANDWICH

40. The Receptionist Hates You for No Good Reason

You say good morning to her every day at 8 A.M. You are always polite when you ask her if you have received any calls. And when she leaves a sticky note on your computer with a message you take the time to personally thank her. And yet, she makes no effort to conceal her hatred toward you. WTF?

The WTF Approach to Dealing with a F*#!-ing Bitch

➤ STEP #1: *Kill Her with Kindness*

Obviously being nice to her has somehow managed to piss her off. So be even nicer if you want to drive her nuts. Bring her coffee every morning and compliment her on how great she looks even when she doesn't. The nicer you are, the more she'll go insane.

➤ STEP #2: *Be a Prick*

Give her the ol' hot and cold. After you've spent some time playing extra nice, be a dick. Women like guys who are pricks and boss them around. Sure she'll complain about you behind your back, but she will secretly develop a liking to you the more you treat her like shit. Remember in high school when the girls always went after the assholes? Trust us; nothing has changed.

Now that you have her wanting you, stick it to her. Everyone knows that if a woman is having a bad day it must mean that she is not sexually satisfied. There is simply no other explanation. Give her all you got and settle her nerves. If all you got is not enough, get a penile implant and try again.

for the ladies . . .

We suggest you skip directly to Step #3, mainly because it would be hot.

WTF: UP CLOSE AND PERSONAL

A coworker and I did our best to kill our boss with kindness. Literally. Our boss, a fat tub of shit with a temper, had one weakness: doughnuts. Even though every time he ate them he would get sick, the gluttonous animal could not help himself when a nice, fresh doughnut was staring him in the face. He just *had* to have it.

So we gave it to him. And gave it to him. And gave it to him. Though it was costing a couple of underpaid financial editors like us a lot of dough, the look on his sweaty face a half hour or so after he devoured a couple of jelly filled treats was priceless.

In all honesty, we were trying to kill him. We figured that sooner or later he would just keel over with a heart attack, a glazed old fashioned sticking out of his rabid mouth.

But he never did. Boston crème, cherry filled, chocolate, glazed, powder, bear claw—there was no doughnut that he could not conquer, no pastry that he could not tame. Despite complaining of sickness minutes after shoving them down his throat, he trudged on, day after day, doughnut after doughnut.

So sadly, despite our efforts, the man lived—albeit with a bad case of diarrhea. Oh well, at least we tried.

—GB

41. You Have to Work with the Boss's Son Who's a Complete Asshole

There's a new member of the team in your department with whom you will be working especially close. He isn't very bright. He isn't very hard working. And he isn't very pleasant to be around. In fact, he's a total asshole. But none of it matters: He is the big boss's son and he's fucking untouchable.

The WTF Approach to Working with the Boss's F*#!-ing Offspring

➤ OPTION #1: *Tattle*

Tell the boss that his son sucks. If everyone else thinks the kid is a total jackass, the dad probably does too. Maybe this is the kid's last chance to straighten up and stop being a dickwad. Who knows, you might find the boss more receptive to your complaints than you think.

➤ OPTION #2: *Get Him Arrested*

Leave a bag of cocaine on his desk, or slip something in his coffee to make him go insane before an important meeting. No matter how close he is with his daddy, the boss will have no choice but to get rid of him if he breaks the law.

▶ OPTION #3: *Befriend Him— Then Destroy Him*

Make friends with him no matter how much of an idiotic asshole he is. Then, once you have earned his trust, convince him that he is better than his father and should run the company. This should be easy since he probably has Daddy issues and a giant chip on his shoulder. Conspire with him to try to sabotage his father. Then, before the plan goes into action, tell his daddy what his son is up to. This will serve to get rid of the wayward asshole while simultaneously getting you in close with the boss. You could even suggest that the boss adopt you as his son to replace that backstabbing prick. Win-win for everyone . . . except for the shithead son.

Work Is No Laughing Matter

"I like work; it fascinates me. I can sit and look at it for hours."

—JEROME K. JEROME

for the ladies . . .

This shouldn't be a problem. You either date the stupid bastard yourself or set him up with your hot friend. Once he starts getting laid he should be easy to manipulate.

IN THE FUTURE . . .

Be born to a powerful man so that you can be the boss's prick son.

42. Someone Is Spreading Rumors About You

The stares, the snickers, the surreptitious whispers behind your back. Did you leave your fly down again? Is there something on your face? Maybe some toilet paper stuck to your shoe? You check yourself out: nothing. But you know something must be up, so what is it? Then your closest ally lets you in on the buzz: Someone is spreading terrible rumors about you throughout the office. But who?

The WTF Approach to Battling the F*#!-ing Office Gossip

> **OPTION #1:** *Fight Fire with Fire*

Spread rumors about everyone in the office. Terrible, vicious rumors. Before you know it everyone will have forgotten the rumors about you entirely.

> **OPTION #2:** *Investigate*

Find out who the culprit is and expose him. Bribe fellow coworkers with coffee and bagels—even offer to take on some of their work. Everyone has a price. Soon you'll discover the source of the rumors. Once exposed, now all you have to do is plan the perfect murder.

➤ OPTION #3: *Embrace Them*

At least people are talking about you. If you are used to being ignored you should embrace your new found infamy. Being so infamous might just get you laid—unless the rumor is that you have no dick.

Rumors: The Bad, the Worse, and the Worst

Some rumors are worse than others. Check out the chart and see how a rumor can go from bad to worst.

BAD	WORSE	WORST
You smell.	You smell like a serial killer—and probably are.	You make perfume out of your victims' blood.
You're addicted to doing drugs.	You're addicted to doing drug dealers.	You're addicted to doing drug dealers who are illegal aliens and have no right to be in our country.
You drank too much at the office Christmas Party.	You drank so much at the office Christmas Party that you tried to blow Santa.	Every lunch break you get gangbanged by a group of angry, well-endowed elves.
You have a small penis.	You have a small penis with a big wart on it.	You have a small penis with a big wart dipped in poop.

43. You Keep Getting Passed Up for a Promotion

Billy got one. Bobby got one. Hell, even that mongoloid, Tom got one. But you? Nothing. Nada. After wasting away most of your twenties in a cubicle all you have is the same paycheck every month—not a dime more than when you started. WTF?

The WTF Approach to Getting What's F*#!-ing Due

> ➤ **OPTION#1: *Move On***

People tend to get stuck in a job and never get out. Don't let that happen to you. People who move up quickly on the corporate ladder seldom do it at the same company. Take a chance, and get the fuck out.

> ➤ **OPTION #2: *Confront Your Boss***

You can do this politely (i.e. address him privately about your grievances) or less politely (i.e. take him by the neck and squeeze). The latter is more fun, but the former will probably yield the better result—unless he's a real hard ass and will appreciate you taking the initiative.

➤ OPTION #3: *Work Harder*

That's right, keep working. Move into your fucking cubicle if you have to. Prove that you deserve that promotion. If you still don't get one then maybe you really suck at your job. Ever think of that, dipshit?

HOW TO ASK FOR A PROMOTION

Should you ask forcefully, or should you appeal to your boss's gentler side? Here's a quiz:

1. When asking for a promotion you should:
   A. Bat your eyes and lick your lips.
   B. Smile like the Cheshire cat.
   C. Look the boss dead in the eye like you want to screw him and/or kill him.
   D. Write down the title and the money you want on a piece of paper and hand it to him so he can laugh in your face.

ANSWER: D. Fucking prick! God, don't you just hate him.

Reasons You're Not Getting Promoted

- You're a slacker.

- You're an asshole.

- You're fat and ugly.

- No one likes you.

for the ladies . . .

Become a man. As sad as it will be to give up benefits like menstruation, pregnancy, and bikini waxing, in a man's world like ours it's your best shot.

44. You Get Wasted and Make an Ass of Yourself at the Christmas Party

Unless you work for *Playboy* or Vivid Video, holiday office parties are usually pretty lame—a pathetic attempt to pretend that people at work actually like each other.

Inevitably this so-called "party" consists of people standing around a table of snacks sipping wine and talking about the only thing they know how to talk about: work.

As a fun-loving optimist, you make the best of a boring situation by doing the only thing you can at a dull event: drink. So you drink, and drink, and drink. The next thing you know you're passed out face down in the middle of the party wearing nothing but your underwear and a Santa hat. Merry Christmas!

The WTF Approach to Doing F*#!-ing Damage Control

➤ **OPTION #1: *Make a Great Speech***

Get up, throw some water in your face and make an incredible, impromptu speech that knocks everyone's socks off. Speak about the company, the direction it needs to go to succeed in today's market, and a moving closing statement about the nature of teamwork. If you don't know shit about the company you work for and have nothing interesting to say, just use the word "synergy" a lot. Using that word always makes you sound like you know what the fuck you are talking about.

➤ **OPTION #2: *Pack a Gat***

Take out a gun and stick a turkey in your shirt. If you have ever seen *Trading Places*, then you know what we are talking about here. If you haven't, then move on to Option #3 fuck-head.

➤ **OPTION #3: *Quit and Get Help***

You'll never live down the embarrassment, no matter how hard you try. When you wake up, leave the building and check yourself into an alcohol rehab center even if you aren't an alcoholic. When you come out, everyone—including your boss—will take pity on you and hire you back. They'll forget all about that night and consider you a hero for taking charge of your life and doing what's best for yourself and the company.

WTFACT: At every company Christmas party there is one drunk asshole. At every company *WTF?* author Gregory Bergman has worked at *he is* that drunk asshole.

45. You Are Your Boss's Secret Santa

It's that time of year again. Snowflakes are falling, Christmas carols have taken over the radio, and militant soldiers from the Salvation Army incessantly ring a bell outside the supermarket in order to drive you insane. Yep, it's Christmas time, and this year it's your turn to give—to your boss.

The WTF Approach to Buying a Gift for the F*#!-ing Man

➤ OPTION #1: *Splurge*

Do not be cheap. If you have to get your kid a pogo stick instead of that red bicycle you promised or your girlfriend/wife a macaroni necklace instead of a tennis bracelet than that's what you are going to do. The last thing you want to do is give your boss yet another reason to can your dumb ass.

➤ OPTION #2: *Do Your Research*

Talk to his wife or girlfriend or boyfriend—whatever the case may be—and find out what he would really like. Don't take any chances. You don't want to get him a nice bottle of Scotch only to find out that he is a recovering alcoholic who has fought like hell to stay sober after that unfortunate accident three years ago when he ran over that woman, her daughter, and their three legged dog.

► OPTION #3: *Quit*

You are underpaid as it is and now the prick is demanding a gift? Get him a card that says "Screw you. I quit!"

Have You Been Naughty or Nice?

Santa is coming to town. Here's a checklist to see if you qualify for a gift or if you will end up empty-handed this Christmas and on your way to hell.

❏ You cheated on your wife with her sister but in your defense it "just happened."

❏ You hit your kid in the head with a shovel but in your defense "he deserved it."

❏ You masturbated to tranny porn but immediately felt awkward and guilty about it.

❏ You spent your family's rent money on crack cocaine but in your defense it totally "ruined your high."

❏ You voted Republican.

We were with you until the last one. But no fucking way are you getting *anything* this year—or ever!

BEST GIFTS FOR THE BOSS	WORST GIFTS FOR THE BOSS
Box of Cuban cigars	Box of Cubans
Bottle of 100-year-old Irish Whiskey	Bottle of 100-year-old Irish peasant piss
Pussy	Pussy cat
Nice watch	Sundial
Money donation to their favorite charity	Money to finance drug relapse

chapter five

romance
in the cubes

46. You Sleep with Your Boss

After months of mutual flirting and innuendo, you end up alone in the conference room late one night with your female boss's ass in your face. After the all-night sex-a-thon, you realize that this night of blissful transgression might have some serious consequences.

The WTF Approach to Banging the Head F*#!-ing Honcho

➤ OPTION #1: *Keep at It*

Hey, it ain't against the law. You've already made your bed, you might as well bang in it.

➤ OPTION #2: *Quit*

Most of the time this ends very badly and not so much for the boss but for the for the poor fool who couldn't keep his dick in his pants—no offense. Better to cut your losses now and move on.

➤ OPTION #3: *Transfer*

Tell her you think you're falling in love with her and it's affecting your work. You might be able to get over her but in order to do that you will have to transfer to another location. Maybe in Hawaii, you should be able to get over her there.

WTF: UP CLOSE AND PERSONAL

If you work in the service industry, screwing the boss is almost a requirement. I was a bartender for thirteen years and I don't think there was one place where I didn't sleep with the owner or a fellow employee. Good times!

—JM

NOTE: Jodi Miller is still really, *really* horny.

IN THE FUTURE . . .

Work for someone ugly—like yourself.

47. The Boss's Hot Wife Wants to Sleep with You

Every time the boss's wife comes into the office, it seems like she's coming to see you. She lingers at your desk, smiles incessantly, and brings you lattes because she thought you might need a little pick-me-up. She also checks you out as you walk away, hungrily leering at your ass cheeks like they're some sort of pastry. Then one day she visits the office while her husband is out of town, comes into your cubicle, and begins to rub your shoulders. "You seem stressed," she whispers. "I bet I could take care of that." Finally, it's abundantly clear: Your boss's hot wife wants your jock.

The WTF Approach to Dealing with Mrs. F*#!-ing Robinson

➤ OPTION #1: *Bang Her*

Duh? Married women have working pussies too, you know. Plus, behind every powerful man is an even more powerful woman. She's the one that probably holds the key to your future. Diddle her good and she could be instrumental in helping to get your promoted. If you diddle her really, really good, she might divorce her husband and win half of his stock in the company in a settlement, making her the largest shareholder. Then she'll fire him and make you the boss.

➤ OPTION #2: *Tell Your Boss*

Just come out and say it. "Sir, um, your wife is . . . well, how to I put this . . . a dirty, filthy, pig of a whore." He might not believe you or he might even blame you for encouraging her, but there's also a chance that you'll earn his trust by outing his wife as a slut.

➤ OPTION #3: *Distract and Deflect*

Find her someone else to hit on. Start sizing up your other coworkers and plant the seeds in her mind that someone else in the office is more worthy of her attention. Say things like, "I heard Steve in Accounting has a 12-inch dick—when it's soft." It's Steve's problem now.

Water Cooler Talk

"Six months into the job, we had a company Christmas party at a hotel. Nearly everyone showed up with a date except for me. I was standing at the bar trying to get as loaded as I possibly could on the company's tab when this hot chick approached me. I was just about to turn on the charm when my boss stepped in front of me and introduced me to her as his wife. Later that evening, when the boss was busy getting his butt kissed by his employees, the horny vixen asked me to join her outside for a smoke. I accepted. After the smoke we went to my car so she could suck on something else, something that had been growing all night. While she was going down on me I began to hear a pounding sound on my windshield. It was my boss screaming at me and threatening to end my life. Well, my life didn't end that night but two other things did: my career with his company and his marriage to his wife."

—Peter Gorman, currently unemployed, but sexually satisfied

48. Your Assistant Is Screwing the Boss

You thought you hired the perfect assistant. She's hard working, compliant, and eager to please. But not anymore. Lately she's slacking off big time. Then you find out that she's not interested in pleasing you because she's too busy pleasing your boss . . . with her vagina. You are now walking a very thin line. The last thing you want to do is piss her off, but you need her to get back to work. She has your future in her hands, or should we say between her legs.

The WTF Approach to Handling a Slutty F*#!-ing Assistant

➤ OPTION #1: *Catch Her In The Act*

Tape it and blackmail your boss. You're missing out on what could be a perfect opportunity to not only create job security, but also advance in the company. Install a mini-camera in his office and tape them doing the deed. Better yet call his wife and have her come down to the office. Then right before she's about to go in and catch them, stop her. Make sure your boss knows you helped out in this sticky situation.

> **OPTION #2: *Report it to HR***

Anonymously of course. Send a note to HR explaining what is going on and let them deal with it. Odds are they will both be let go. At least your assistant will, and maybe your boss will be transferred. Either way you will be in the clear and get a new assistant.

> **OPTION #3: *Do Nothing***

Just because she can suck a dick, doesn't mean she's good enough with clients to take over your job. Unless, of course, she's *really good* at sucking dick.

> **OPTION #4: *Follow Her Lead***

Fuck it, fight fire with fire. Start nailing the boss's assistant. Hopefully you can get some dirt on your boss while you're at it.

GILF (Grandmother I'd Like to F*#!) Alert

Careful, usually the boss's assistant has been with him for years. She's likely some sixty-year-old grandma you wouldn't want to bang . . . would you?

Hottest GILFs

* Sarah Palin
* Goldie Hawn
* Sophia Loren
* Helen Mirren
* That old white-haired woman who's at the Santa Monica Boulevard bus stop every morning with that cane and those tits . . . you know who you are.

49. You Have a Reputation for Being a Man Whore

When you were in college, screwing everything that moved was par for the course. But in corporate America, sleeping with anything with a pulse is less acceptable. So after making your way through all your female coworkers you are now officially the most infamous man whore in company history—and everyone knows it.

The WTF Approach to Clearing Up Your F*#!-ing Reputation

➤ OPTION #1: *Do Nothing*

It's not your fault. Claim that you are a sex addict and that you are seeking treatment. Having an addiction is very trendy right now. Also, they won't be able to fire you if you claim you are seeking help for this disease. People will sympathize with you. Shit, you'll probably get some sympathy pussy out of the deal too. But don't feel bad, relapsing is an important part of recovery.

➤ OPTION #2: *Flip the Switch*

Tell everyone that you're not the whore, all these women are. You just want to come in, do your work, and go home. But the way these women dress nowadays with their shirts and their pants is more than any man can take. Not to mention their seductive "good mornings" and "have a good nights." For Christ's Sake, what's a red-blooded American guy to do?

➤ OPTION #3: *Stop Being a Whore*

Keep your dick in your pants. You're not an animal. Wait 'til after work then go pick up some trash at your local bar.

Biggest Man Whores in History

- Wilt Chamberlain
- Don Juan
- Colin Farrell
- Bill Clinton
- Henry VIII

You Might Be a Man Whore If . . .

❑ On bring your kid to work day, half the kids are yours.

❑ You can't trace the STDs you've contracted this year to the corresponding department, let alone the girl.

❑ There's a condom dispenser on your desk.

❑ Your desk drawer has more pairs of panties than Victoria's Secret.

❑ When you are introduced by a coworker, you're referred to simply as "Whore."

50. You Get Caught Having Sex in the Supply Closet with the UPS Chick

You had a feeling that cute UPS girl had the hots for you. Every time you go to sign for a package, she's checking out yours. Then one day, when you ask her to hold the package so you can sign it she says, "I'd love to" and grabs your balls instead. A few minutes later you crazy kids are playing hide the salami in the supply closet. That is, until Mary from Accounting busts in looking for a box of pens.

The WTF Approach to Getting Caught with Your F*#!-ing Pants Down

➤ **OPTION #1:** *Cry Rape*

Start screaming and throw the UPS gal off your lap. Thank Mary for saving you from this mad woman who violently pounced on you. It might not be easy to explain how she managed to force you to go into the supply closet, take out your penis, and give it to her from behind but if you scream loud enough people might buy it.

➤ **OPTION #2:** *Propose*

That's right; drop to your knees and ask the UPS girl to be your

wife. Sure she'll be totally confused and completely freaked out,
but Mary will think she just witnessed a very romantic moment
and might not even notice that you
were just balls deep in her ass.
Mazel tov!

➤ OPTION #3: *Keep Going*

You might as well. You're probably
going to get fired for this so you
might as well go out with a bang.
Literally.

➤ OPTION #4: *Ask Her to Join*

She might just surprise you. After
all, what happens in the supply
closet stays in the supply closet.

for the ladies . . .

If you get caught screwing the UPS
guy in the supply closet, we would like
to offer you a job—immediately.

Best Places to Have Sex at Work

* Janitor's closet

* Boss's desk

* Conference room table

Worst Places to Have Sex at Work

* In the incinerator

* On the fax machine

* Inside a coffee mug

51. Everyone Is Having Sex Except You

You can't take it anymore; everyone in your office is getting laid except you! The receptionist and the boss. The boss and the office manager. The office manager and the freckle-faced kid from Tech Support. The freckle-faced kid in Tech Support and the Marketing Director. The Marketing Director and the receptionist (that one was particularly hot!). Your office is just one big orgy—and you're not invited.

The WTF Approach to Getting Some F*#!-ing Ass

> **STEP #1: *Eliminate the Competition***

Spread rumors about the competition. If there are one or two really popular guys who seem to be banging most of the girls in the office, do your best to cock block them by spreading vicious rumors. Remember, herpes may not be desirable but you can live with it. AIDS on the other hand will really make a chick think twice—no matter how chiseled the dude's abs are.

> **STEP #2: *Get a Makeover***

Become sexier and/or more interesting. Obviously you're doing something wrong. If you are ugly, become funny and charming. If you are fat, lose weight. And if you are a pussy, grow some balls and get laid.

> STEP #3: *Make a Statement*

Wear pink or something outrageous. It's called "peacocking," and many of the so-called "gurus" and pick up artists swear by it. The theory here is that it is always better to stand out, even if you look like a jackass, because it draws women's attention to you. If you really can't pull off pink because you are still too fat and ugly, try a lighter shade of purple —and shove a big sock in your pants.

> STEP #4: *Find an Easy Target*

Go after the most promiscuous one. (Hint: It's probably the one you least expect.) You know, the girl with glasses and no makeup who dresses weird and eats alone in the corner during lunchtime, daydreaming about unicorns, magic castles and fat cocks.

WTFACT: Seventeen percent of respondents in a 2007 Vault.com survey admit to being caught trysting on the job.

F*#! Work, Let's F*#!

Two court clerks in Barberton, Ohio were caught having sex in the storage room above the courtroom. The story was such a sensation that it made the front page of *The Barberton Herald*, one of the most widely circulated and prestigious periodicals in the nation.

52. Your Coworker Tapes Your Sexual Encounter

Happy hour was better than expected this time around. You had been flirting with that chick from Marketing the past few times you went out, but this time you finally got a chance to be alone with her. After some initial groping in the bar, you find yourself in her bed looking up at her perfect breasts. Life just doesn't get better than this.

But it *does* get worse. The next morning, you find out why she kept going to adjust something on her computer as she screwed you. That's right. She was recording your little session. WTF?

The WTF Approach to Getting F*#!-ing Revenge

➤ STEP #1: *Confront Her*

Find out what she wants. Maybe she wants to blackmail you. Maybe she wants to embarrass you. Or maybe she is just a sick fucking pervert who loves to show off her sex skills to millions of viewers around the world. Whatever her motivation, find out what this twisted bitch wants before she starts sending links to everyone in the office.

> **STEP #2: *Get Her Fired***

Before the little perv chick can blackmail you, take it to your boss, claim that she drugged you and taped the encounter in hopes of bringing down the company. In fact there's a good possibility that loose lips is a spy. She'll be canned immediately.

> **STEP #3: *Embrace It***

Chances are she's going to get back at you for getting her fired by releasing the tape. What's the matter, afraid everyone is going to see your little pee pee? Hey, if you got nothing to be embarrassed about then why the fuck do you care if half the country sees you giving a Dirty Sanchez? Remember, anyone who sees you obviously watches that shit so they can't judge.

Famous Sex Tapes

- Tommy Lee and Pamela Anderson

- Paris Hilton and everyone

- Charlie Brown and Peppermint Patty (animated)

- JFK and Marilyn Monroe (only available in 8mm)

- Abraham Lincoln and Mary Todd (only available in sketch drawings)

- Adam and Eve (only available in Bibles)

DIY Porno

Here are some helpful tips for making a good sex tape:

1. Get good lighting

2. Spray tan

3. Practice your moves in the mirror before taping

4. Set the tone with some mood music

5. Get a great editor (This is the most important. If you cum too soon, your editor will be able to drag that shit out so you look like a pro.)

53. The Security Guard Catches You Screwing on Tape

After months of flirtation, you finally have your sexy coworker right where you want her—on your dick. Who would have known that working late on a project could be so much fun? But the next day you find yourself screwed again—and not in a good way. Turns out that the copies you made of her ass on the copy machine aren't the only evidence of that wild night—there's a friggin' tape, and the security guy has got it.

The WTF Approach to Getting Back Your F*#!-ing Sex Tape

➤ **OPTION #1: *Tell Him to Fuck Off***

Hey, if you're a single guy and your boss is a cool dude then the security guy has nothing on you. Who cares if he has a tape of your flabby ass porking some broad on the boardroom table? Tell him to enjoy the tape because that's about as close as a fat loser like him will ever get to a nice piece of ass.

➤ **OPTION #2: *Give in to His Demands***

Give the security prick what he wants if he's got you by the balls. You don't want him sending the tape to your girlfriend. Nor do you want your uptight boss to find out your unique definition of "overtime." Pay the schmuck and be done with it.

➤ OPTION #3: *Flip the Switch*

Agree to pay the security pig but stall him for a few days by telling him that you are waiting for a check to clear. Meanwhile, tell your coworker what is going on and devise a plan to destroy him. Have her come in late one night in a trench coat and nothing else and seduce him while you hide and get it on tape with your camcorder. Now *you* are in a position to blackmail *him*. Even better, you are in a position to blackmail them both.

Sex Tapes That Have Advanced Careers

* Kim Kardashian

* Paris Hilton

* Tommy Lee

* ~~Verne Troyer~~

* Brett Michaels

* Colin Farrell

* Madonna

* ~~Dustin Diamond~~

for the ladies . . .

Hot! Burn copies and sell that shit!

54. Your Coworker Catches You Masturbating at Your Desk

Normally, you whack off in the morning and before bed, just like any other horny animal. But lately you've been working so late that you don't have the energy to spank your monkey when you get home, which is starting to affect your sleep. So one night when you're alone in the office pounding away at your computer in your cubicle, you take a break and decide to pound your cock instead. Then the unthinkable happens: One of your coworkers walks in and sees you treating your penis like a hand puppet.

The WTF Approach to Getting Caught with Your Hand Down Your F*#!-ing Pants

➤ OPTION #1: *Ask for Assistance*

She might go for it. Just explain to her that part of being a team player is working together with your fellow coworkers to achieve a specific goal. Does it matter if the "goal" in mind here is ejaculating all over the recently steamed carpets?

➤ OPTION #2: *Give a Sob Story*

Tell the coworker that your wife/ girlfriend doesn't sleep with you anymore. If you have a small penis, show her and then start to cry. She'll understand.

> ► **OPTION #3:** *Finish*

Explain that you need to do this in order to work your best. You find that after a giant release you are more relaxed and get more work done. Then suggest that she give it a try.

WTF: UP CLOSE AND PERSONAL

As a chronic masturbator, I have probably squandered a third of my free time since puberty looking at pornography and masturbating. For a while I really couldn't stop, and had to masturbate wherever I was—including the office.

When I was bored at work, I browsed porn on the Internet, glancing over my shoulder periodically to see if I my superiors were watching. Hiding away in my cubicle, I would play with myself through my pants until I was ready to ejaculate. Having been raised with very strict parents, I would not dream of actually letting loose all over my desk during business hours. That would be in poor taste. Fully and painfully erect, I would stand up from my desk with a raging hard on, using a folder of some sort to hide the bulge in my pants as I made my way past my coworkers and the suspicious receptionist to the comfortable solace of a bathroom stall.

There, on the frigid toilet seat, I would desperately recall the porn clip, and jerk off for the second time of the day . . . and this was before lunch.

And that's how I roll, dawg.
—GB

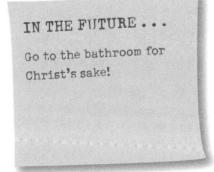

IN THE FUTURE . . .

Go to the bathroom for Christ's sake!

55. You Sleep with the Client and Lose the Account

Well, now you've really gone and done it. While we're proud that you finally got laid, did you really have to screw your client? Screwing a client metaphorically is one thing (it's expected), but *literally*? This can only lead to trouble. Now you've lost the account, and maybe even your job.

The WTF Approach to Saving Your F*#!-ing Ass

➤**OPTION #1: *Reason with Her***

Tell your client that you are sorry for whatever you did to offend her and that you promise it will be just business from now on.

➤**OPTION #2: *Pass Her Off***

Get her assigned to another agent. You may not be able to save your pride, but you can still save your job. Just because you suck in bed, doesn't mean there

isn't someone at Moron & Moron, LLP who can handle her properly. When in doubt, approach the black guy in the office. You know, the one with the really, really big desk.

➤**OPTION #3: *Become a Eunuch***

You're obviously unfit for polite society and have to be stopped. Screwing your own client? You animal! You monster! Castrate yourself and end your sexual cravings. The safety of the civilized world depends on it.

Top Five Professions Where Screwing Clients Is Expected

1. Porn star

2. Prostitute

3. Masseuse

4. Sex therapist

5. Attorney

Top Ten Worse Things to Hear During Sex

1. "What's your name?"

2. "Do you smell something really, really bad?"

3. "I have something to confess: I am your real mother."

4. "Faster, slower, harder, to the left, no scratch that, to the right . . ."

5. "Mind if I shit on you now?"

6. "If a train is leaving from Boston headed West and another train is leaving from San Francisco headed East . . ."

7. "Look at me. Please, baby, look at me."

8. "Is it in yet?"

9. "Ha, ha. Oh my God, really? It is in? No way!"

10. "I love you."

IN THE FUTURE . . .

Get better in bed. Obviously you need to up your game. Read *Cosmo* to find out how to make a woman swoon, start taking penile enhancement pills, and strengthen your tongue by trying to touch the tip to your nose.

chapter six

you're
the boss

56. You Have to Fire Someone You Like

Firing someone is tough—but even tougher when it's a friend. You know his sad little story and don't want to be the one to crush his hopes and his dreams. And no matter how you go about canning him, he's going to blame and resent you. Remember the time you banged his mom? This is just like that—but less gross.

The WTF Approach to Firing a F*#!-ing Friend

➤ OPTION #1: *Distract and Deflect*

Fire him and take him to Vegas. It's the cure for the blues. Break the news Friday afternoon and, after he starts to cry, tell him you've booked a hotel and several escorts at Caesar's. A Jacuzzi party with prostitutes can make anyone forget about anything.

➤ OPTION #2: *Make Him Quit*

If you are too cowardly to do the deed, start piling on the work and blame it on the guys at the top. Say your hands are tied and if he wants to keep his job he'll will have to stay late and work weekends, even work on Christmas day. We give it a month. Then when he threatens to quit tell him, as a friend, if you fire him he'll get a severance package. Now it's on him.

➤ OPTION #3: *Inflate His Ego*

Convince him that this job is preventing him from living up to his full potential. "You're better than this," tell him. Explain to him you always thought he deserved much more out of life, and that he should follow his dreams. Remind him of that funny drawing he did of the teacher in junior high. Then tell him that drawing comics is where the money is.

➤ OPTION #4: *Just Do It*

Pack up his shit and leave it at the front door. Then make sure security knows not to let him in. He'll get the hint. Cruel maybe, but at least you won't have to do it face to face, pussy!

Think Before You Fire

The best way to fire a friend:

Boss: Sorry to do this but I am going to have to let you go.

Employee Friend: Oh, my God! How will I get by?!

Boss: Not my problem, loser. Vegas on me?

The worst way to fire a friend:

Boss: Beat it.

Employee Friend: What?

Boss: Pack your shit and get the fuck out of here before I call security. And by the way, I fucked your wife.

(*Door Slam*)

57. You Get No Respect

You've worked like a dog, paid your dues, and now you are a big boss making the big bucks. But no matter how far you climb up the corporate ladder, your underlings give you no respect. They come in when they want. They leave when they want. They sometimes don't come in at all. What the fuck? It's time for you to man up and make your minions do as they're told.

The WTF Approach to Not Being a F*#!-ing Doormat

> ➤ **OPTION #1: *Start Firing***

Machiavelli was right when he said it is better to be feared than loved. So start chopping heads. That will send a crystal clear signal to everyone that you're not fucking around. Watch them line up to kiss your ass!

> ➤ **OPTION #2: *Throw a Party***

Get tons of booze and throw an all-out bash. Show everyone just how cool you real are.

> ➤ **OPTION #3: *Start Small***

Just get one on your side. Although we're no longer in high school the same rules apply. If one of the popular kids likes you everyone else will follow their lead. Get the most popular person in the office to be your friend and everyone else should follow suit. If you don't know how to get that one person on your side go with Option #2.

Top Five Worst Bosses

1. Naomi Campbell

2. Christian Bale

3. Henry VIII (especially if you were married to him)

4. Ebenezer Scrooge

5. Any white person during slavery

58. Everyone Hates You

It would be one thing if you were the big boss, in which case it would be somewhat expected. But you are just a mid-level schmuck and everyone—no matter what you seem to do—hates your guts. The sneers, the whispers, and complete avoidance; it's all just getting to be too much to bear. Everyone in the office wants you dead. What the fuck did you do wrong?

The WTF Approach to Managing People Who Hate Your F*#!-ing Guts

➤ OPTION #1: *Stop Giving a Fuck*

So what if everyone hates you? Stop worrying about it like a pussy. People can smell that insecurity. The minute you stop giving a fuck about making friends people will start trying to befriend *you*.

➤ OPTION #2: *Bribe Them*

Bring bagels and coffee. Even if you have already tried this, try again. Bring bagels and coffee and whatever everyone wants every day and eventually people will like you—if only for the bagels and coffee.

NOTE: Your desperation will be obvious and people will laugh and mock you behind your back, but at least they'll pretend to like you.

Are You an Asshole?

If everyone hates you, you might be too much of a prick. Take this quiz to find out just how big of a douche bag you are:

1. When you are greeted with a "Good morning" you usually:

   A. Say good morning back.

   B. Nod your head in recognition of the kind gesture but say nothing.

   C. Keep walking and completely ignore the bitch.

   D. Tell the person to go fuck himself.

2. When one of your fellow managers gets chewed out by the boss, you:

   A. Add insult to injury by insulting his ethnic back ground and calling his mom a "whore bucket."

   B. Get him wasted after work so he can drown his sorrows.

   C. Say nothing and do nothing. He is beneath you both in the company hierarchy and in the hierarchy of human life.

3. When a coworker is having trouble with an assignment and asks for help, you:

   A. Charge him a side fee.

   B. Tell the boss immediately that he is an idiot and cannot do the job himself and should therefore be canned.

   C. Laugh maniacally and spit in his face.

ANSWER EVALUATION:

1. If you answered:

   A. You are a really nice dude. Way to be, brah!

   B. You are either not a morning person or are really shy, but not necessarily a total asshole.

   C. You are an asshole, but in a cool kind of way.

   D. You are a fucking asshole in desperate need of anger management classes.

2. If you answered:

   A. You are a real scumbag. Come on, making fun of his race *and* his mother?

   B. You are a good guy, a real pal.

   D. You are an asshole—and not in a cool way. Watch yourself. You might have tendencies that could result in a blood bath.

3. If you answered:

   A. You are a prick, but again in a cool way.

   B. You are a little bitch asshole, not a man at all.

   C. You are a fucking psycho.

59. You Have to Lay Off the Whole Division

It's good to be the boss. You make more money, people constantly kiss your ass, and you can basically do as you please. But, unless you are a sadistic animal, there is one time when being a boss sucks balls: When you have to can someone and put them out on the street.

Letting someone go is tough enough, but when you hear you have to lay off an entire division, you can barely catch your breath. Have fun, boss man!

The WTF Approach to Firing a Lot of F*#!-ing People

➤ OPTION #1· *Sugarcoat It*

Send them all to a baseball game. Don't spend a lot on the walking dead, so maybe something in the nose bleed section. Then, during the seventh inning stretch, pay to have the words "YOU'RE ALL FIRED" on the JumboTron screen. At first they might start laughing, feeling sorry for whoever that was directed to. But they'll get the hint when they see the next message with your company logo and the words, "THAT MEANS YOU, MORON!" Grab a hot dog and a beer to cheer yourself up. You had an emotional day, after all.

➤ OPTION #2: *Move the Rest of Your Company*

Pick up and move the rest of your people to another office building without telling that division. Change your name and number.

> **NOTE:** If this happens to you, see "Your Company Suddenly Relocates without Telling You" (Page 211).

➤ OPTION #3: *Shift the Blame*

Call them in one by one and explain that you have to let the division go because of one of their coworkers. Tell Steven it's because of Bob. Then call Bob in and blame it on Paula. Then call in Paula and blame it on Steven. You get the point. They'll be so pissed at each other they won't have any energy to blame you.

60. You Knock Up Your Coworker

You ignored all the warnings when you started sleeping with your coworker. You are never supposed to dip your pen in the company ink, right? Too late. And if that isn't bad enough, you notice she's running to the bathroom every morning to throw up and her clothes are getting tighter by the day. Then she breaks the news: "I'm pregnant, baby and you're the father. Congrats!"

Holy fucking shit.

The WTF Approach to Being a F*#!-ing Daddy

➤ STEP #1: *Abort*

Offer to pay to get rid of the problem. Explain to her she has a brilliant career as a receptionist ahead of her and she shouldn't let an unplanned pregnancy get in the way.

NOTE: If you are against abortion, then pray for a miscarriage. Chances are you are religious, so maybe God will do you a solid.

➤ STEP #2: *Become an Alcoholic*

If she doesn't go for the quick out, start drinking and don't stop. Sure you might loose your job, your friends, and your self-worth, but she'll soon realize she can't have a drunk around her kid. You'll be saving a shit-load of money that you can now use for rehab. Smart move.

➤ **STEP #3:** *Deny It*

Then get really mad and accuse her of sleeping with some other guy. Worst case you wind up on *Maury* and she proves it's yours. At least you got to be on TV.

➤ **STEP #4:** *Use It*

If you still haven't driven her away, just go with it. Sometimes both the mother and father get paid leave when a baby is born. So hang in there until she gives birth then enjoy your paid vacation while your baby's mama does all the hard work. As soon as she realizes what a deadbeat dad you are, she'll release you of any parental obligations. Win, win—except for the kid.

WTF? HR Department

Pregnant women are hot messes. Therefore, there are a few things you should never say to a pregnant coworker:

- Are you *sure* that you're not having twins? Really?

- Your belly would be hot if it were a tit or something instead of a fat stomach

- Where does the fetus' pee and poop go?

- Do you know who the father is?

- It must be really hard looking like such a fat, repugnant pig, huh?

61. You Crash the Company Car

Work life, even at the top, has very few perks: a membership to a country club, a parking spot right in the front, a sexy secretary willing to start off your mornings with a customary hand job, or, for the really lucky, a company car that you don't have to pay for.

After years of slaving away for the company, you are finally given a company car. For months now you've been living like a fat cat, driving the pimped out new Mercedes on the company's dime. Life could not get any better. That is, until you wreck the fucking thing and tear it in half. Shit, your boss is going to kill you.

The WTF Approach to Covering Up Your F*#!-ing Crash

➤ **OPTION #1: Hide the Evidence**

Sell the car for scrap and then call in to work and say that you were carjacked. Tell a harrowing story about a guy dressed in black with a gun. They'll just be happy that you're alive.

➤ **OPTION #2: Set the Car on Fire**

Set the car on fire and dance around it like a complete lunatic, laughing maniacally. Then get a paid leave of absence for a mental breakdown. It's better than working, anyway.

➤ **OPTION #3:** *Flip the Switch*

Tell them that there was something wrong with the brakes and that they didn't work when you tried to stop. Scream and carry on to your bosses that they put your life in danger by giving you this crappy car. Make enough of a fuss and they'll end up apologizing to *you*.

WTFACT: The first automobile-related fatality occurred in London in 1896. After that the coroner said: "This must never happen again." It did.

IN THE FUTURE . . .

Take your eyes off your BlackBerry and look at the fucking road, asshole.

Things You Should Never Do While Driving

* Get a manicure

* Get a pedicure

* Read the paper

* Floss

* Cook

WHAT THE F*#! IS UP WITH . . .
TEXTING AND DRIVING

It's one thing to be on the phone and driving, but quite another to be texting and going 60 mph in that hunk of metal filled with gas called an automobile. What are you, a fucking idiot? How can you drive if you can't see? Newsflash for all you texting drivers out there: Messaging back "K" to a text from your girlfriend about having chicken and rice for dinner (again) isn't exactly worth dying for.

62. Your Parking Spot Is Given to Someone Else

There are a few little things that keep all of us going to work, things that make life at the office just a little less horrible. Things like free coffee and bagels in the morning, a cubicle or office we can decorate as we see fit, and, of course, a parking space to call your own. Take away one of these perks and the full scale of your miserable life hits you smack in the face. So the day you drive into the lot and realize they've taken your parking spot away and given it to someone else, you're ready to lose your shit.

The WTF Approach to Dealing with Losing Your F*#!-ing Space

➤ OPTION #1: Fuck It

Just keep parking there. Get in early every day and park your car in your old spot before the prick gets to work. Who knows, the bosses might even give it back to you for working so hard and coming in early. Maybe all they wanted from you was a renewed commitment to the job, the same gusto and tenacity that you brought to the position years ago.

➤ **OPTION #2:** *Go Gangster*

Throw the prick that got your spot down the stairs. Hopefully, he'll break his neck. This way you'll get your spot back because when he eventually gets released from the hospital and goes back to work, he'll get a handicapped spot right in the front. Win-win for everyone!

➤ **OPTION #3:** *Break Your Own Neck*

Fuck it. That handicapped spot really is *right* in front. It's worth it.

What Your Car Says About You

Cars make a statement about the driver. Here are some examples on what the car says about the driver.

Volkswagen Bug: Old hippy if it's the old version; young chick or gay man if it's the new one

Cadillac Escalade: Violent gang member

New Volvo: Yuppie scumbag who can't afford a BMW or Mercedes

Old Volvo: Pervert and/or kindergarten teacher

Bentley: Basketball player, movie star, or financial criminal

Maserati: Asshole who can't afford a Bentley

BMW: Asshole who can't afford a Maserati

Land Rover: British dickhead

Van: Plumber and/or rapist

Harley Davidson: Genuine scumbag or Yuppie pretending to be a genuine scumbag

Hummer: Man born without a penis

Mitsubishi Eclipse: Hot young co-ed with tits so big that she almost looks deformed—in a good way

Chrysler 300: Middle-class professional who wants to fool you into thinking it's a Bentley if you look really, really fast

IN THE FUTURE . . .

Ride a motorcycle so you never have to worry about parking. It might make a nerdy douche bag like you look cooler, too.

63. You Spread a Disease Throughout Your Office

You wake up one morning feeling like shit. Sore throat, sneezing, coughing, fever but you used up all of your sick days last week when you went to Vegas . . . fuck! And it turns out the old adage "What happens in Vegas stays in Vegas" isn't always true. Looks like you came back with a new strain of flu—the dog flu. (Guess you shouldn't have screwed that golden retriever behind the dumpster next to the souvenir shop.)

Though you feel terrible, you *have* to go to work. Somehow you make it through the day without passing out at your desk, or crying. And then within a week you're feeling better. But as you get better, your coworkers get sicker and sicker. Looks like they all have the dog flu because some asshole spread the virus throughout the whole company.

The WTF Approach to Handling a F*#!-ing Office Epidemic

> **OPTION #1:** *Benefit from It*

Since most of the employees are out sick, take this opportunity to show your strength. Work double time, take on more responsibilities, and who knows, you might just wind up with a promotion out of it.

> **OPTION #2:** *Own It*

Take the credit for all the damage and don't apologize. Fuck them and their weak immune systems.

> **OPTION #3:** *Make It Worse*

Give them something to really complain about. Go out and find someone with leprosy whose skin is hanging off and show all of your coworkers what a real disease can do. They should be lucky it's just the dog flu and quite their bitching. At least their flesh is still on their bones.

IN THE FUTURE . . .

Don't have sex with dogs . . . no matter how good that golden coat looks at 5 A.M. after a three-night binge.

WTF HEALTH TIPS

In order to keep your office environment clean of germs and infections, here are a few pointers on what's okay to spread—and what isn't.

Things You Should Spread

- Love
- Good will
- The Word of God
- Peanut butter on your dick

Things You Should *Never* Spread

- Rumors (unless you hate that person)
- Herpes
- Ebola
- Peanut butter on someone else's dick

chapter seven

blue collar
jobs

64. You're a Cop and Can't Remember the Codes

You made it through the academy. Somehow managed to pass the physical and psychological exam, and just slipped by on the written. Now your childhood dream of being able to shoot and kill gang members has finally come true. You can't wait to get your feet wet—and shoot a Crip in the face. But there is one problem: You can't seem to remember the codes. You're the dumbest cop on the beat—and that's saying something.

The WTF Approach to Remembering those F*#!-ing Codes

➤ OPTION #1: *Watch* Cops

Sit down and watch a marathon of the show *Cops*. They rattle off codes every thirty seconds. Just fake it 'til you make it.

➤ OPTION #2: *Carry a Cheat Sheet*

That's probably how you passed most of your tests in school. Just write the codes down on a piece of paper and pull it out when you need it. But be careful. No one is going to wait for you to find the correct code before they blow you away.

➤ OPTION #3: *Get Shot*

Not somewhere fatal, try the leg or the shoulder. This way you will get a paid leave while you recuperate, giving you ample time to learn those codes. If you still can't remember any codes after this ordeal and your paid leave, tell your superior you have posttraumatic stress syndrome from the shooting and you want to be transferred to a desk job. This would be called A-19. Translation: I am a fucking pussy.

➤ OPTION #4: *Make Up Your Own*

So what if you call in a high-speed chase when there's just a cat in a tree? To those poor cat-loving kids, it's just as urgent.

CODES *NOT* USED BY LAW ENFORCEMENT

Here are a few codes that are too complicated to be used by law enforcement professionals:

- DaVinci Code
- The Code of Hammurabi
- The Bro Code

IN THE FUTURE . . .

Don't be a cop. The pay sucks and you only get to kill people once in a while.

65. You Fall Off the Scaffold

When you told your friends and family you would be working on a scaffold they had some concerns. Namely, why the fuck are you working on a scaffold when you graduated at the top of your class? Not to mention you're a notorious klutz and you're afraid of heights. It was only a matter of time before the inevitable happened. What a jerk.

The WTF Approach to Surviving as a F*#!-ing Klutz

➤ OPTION #1: *Sue*

We smell a hefty law suit. Even though it was your fault, blame it on the scaffold manufacturer. They'll probably settle out of court and you could make millions and never have to work again. True you'll miss scaffolding, but you'll find other, equally fun things to do with your free time and big money—like screw supermodels in a pile of cash.

➤ OPTION #2: *Become Religious*

If you survived the fall, God must really like you. So get on your knees and start praying, asshole. This is your second chance to be a good person and stop being such a jackass.

NOTE: We are assuming that you are a jackass because only a fucking jackass would fall off a scaffold.

➤ OPTION #3: *Shake It Off*

You don't want everyone to think you're a pussy do you? Pick up your mangled body and what's left of your dignity and get back to work!

Most Dangerous Jobs

- Firefighter
- Police officer
- Convenience store clerk
- Commercial fisherman
- First Black president

Creepiest Jobs

- Mortician
- Grave digger
- Taxidermist
- Mickey Rourke's makeup artist
- Michael Jackson's dermatologist . . . especially now

WTF: UP CLOSE AND PERSONAL

I used to have rock fights with my friends after school as a kid. One day, like the idiot I was, I stood on top of a roof that I was supposed to be sweeping (little after school gig), and started a rock fight with a couple kids. Standing on the edge, I reveled in sadistic delight as I pummeled them with rocks, like an Arab throwing a stone at an adulterer. And then, as quickly as it began, the fun stopped. Hit in the knee cap with a sharp rock, I tumbled to the ground, smashing my head onto the cement. Good times.

—GB

MOST UNNECESSARY JOBS

- Adult film screenwriter
- Bathroom attendant
- Congressman
- The Pope
- Bum with dirty windshield wiper who you keep telling to "get the fuck off my car!"

66. You're a Big City Construction Worker and You're Afraid of Heights

Aw, poor wittle baby is awfwaid of being high in the sky wiffout something to secure him from falling to his deaf? Pussy. If you're stupid enough to take a job as a construction worker in the city then you're going to have to deal with this little problem and fast, 'cause the city never sleeps, bitch.

The WTF Approach to Dealing with Your F*#!-ing Fear

➤ OPTION #1: *Become a Mohawk*

Mohawks are a particularly brave Native American tribe when it comes to working on skyscrapers. Known as "skywalkers," Mohawk Indian ironworkers contributed greatly to the construction of the Empire State Building and other famed New York City skyscrapers.

➤ OPTION #2: *Become a Man*

Come on, pussy boy. What's the worst that can happen? Oh, yeah . . . never mind.

➤ OPTION #3: *Become a Suburbanite*

You can get a job working on constructing fast food restaurants or single story houses. The big city construction world is just not for you.

➤ OPTION #4: *Get Drunk*

Have a few beers. It'll loosen you up.

IN THE FUTURE . . .

Get a degree so you can take a desk job, asshole.

CONQUER YOUR FEARS

One way is to undergo hypnotherapy. It might help you get over your fear of heights, just like it can get people to quit smoking and make a woman deliver a baby without feeling a thing. Have the hypnotist convince you that you are brave, instead of the little bitch that you really are. Most of the times our fears are the product of a traumatic experience. For instance, if your dad beat the shit out of you, you might have a phobia of getting the shit beat out of you by your dad.

Another (cheaper) way is to face your fears head on. If you are afraid of heights, go somewhere high and jump. Careful, not too high, though . . . no!

67. You're the Only English-Speaking Person in the Kitchen

You finally got your dream job as a cook in the back of some smelly diner. You love it. After all, who wouldn't? But there is only one problem: No one understands you and you have no idea what the hell anyone else is saying. Hello— does anyone here speak *American*?! WTF?

The WTF Approach to Siendo el único Que Habla F*#!-ing Inglés
(Being the Only One Who Speaks F*#!-ing Inglés)

➤ **OPTION #1:** *Use Sign Language*

Maybe not the official sign language, like in the deaf community but the kind that even a moron can understand to cover the important things like, "you wash dish," "you cook food," "you suck cock."

➤ **OPTION #2:** *Learn Their Language*

Odds are it's probably Spanish, and that shit is pretty easy to learn. If you can't beat 'em, join 'em.

➤ OPTION #3: *Call INS*

Get all your cooking coworkers deported. Now you are not the only the English-speaking person in the kitchen. You're the only person in the kitchen. Looks like you'll be getting a raise.

for the ladies . . .

Doesn't really matter if you can't communicate with anyone in the kitchen. Everyone is staring at your tits anyway.

68. You're a Construction Worker and You Don't Know How to Cat Call

When you tell people you work in construction they immediately know three things about you. You like beer for lunch, you make decent money, and your idea of a charming pickup line is shouting obscenities from a scaffold five floors up to a woman walking down below. In short, people just assume that you are a fucking moron bent on terrorizing neighborhood women who walk by the site. But the problem is that, unlike your coworkers, you're a shy little pussy who can't even approach a woman at a brothel, let alone call out to a stranger on her way to work.

The WTF Approach to Becoming One of the F*#!-ing Guys

➤ OPTION #1: *Follow the Leader*

Just repeat whatever your fellow workers are saying. If they say, "Hey baby, you need me to patch up your hole?" You say, "Yeah, patch up that hole." Be like the big, fat sidekick in the movie that just says "yeah" after everything the other guys says.

➤OPTION #2: *Say Nothing*

You probably will be even creepier if you just stare at them intensely with a look that says, "I would love to have sex with you or kill you . . . either way." Women love intense men.

➤OPTION #3: *Try a Different Approach*

If you don't feel comfortable mimicking the usual crude construction worker gibberish, give your favorite lines from famous romantic comedies your own twist and yell them out such as: "You had me at phat ass jiggling down the street" or "This is one afternoon you are not turning me down" or, our personal favorite, "Here's looking at you, bitch." Women love romance.

What's Up with Cat Calling Anyway?

When did this begin? Did it start back in Egypt when the slaves were building the pyramids and they saw a young lady walk by? Did they yell out things like "Walk like an Egyptian, girl!" "You're making me as stiff as a mummy, baby!" or "Who's your Pharaoh?" And what was this first jackass really thinking? Did he really think that if he shouted something offensive and degrading the woman walking 200 feet below would drop her pants, bend over, and beg him to rail her? Here's a tip construction bozos: Stop screaming stupid shit and get back to work.

Classic Cat Calls

- "Hey mutha want a nutha!?"

- "Hey baby, why don't you lose your little brother and come hang out with a real man!"

- "I heard you lost your virginity . . . can I have the box it came in?"

- "There's a party in my pants, and you're invited!"

- "Lose the zero and get with the hero!"

- "See this 2" × 4"? It's got nothing on my cock!"

for the ladies . . .

- "You wanna show me your *hard* hat?"

- "Wanna *drill* me?"

- "Wanna go on lunch break and see what's in my *box*?"

NOTE: If you use any of the above suggestions you are, by definition, a whore.

69. You're a Firefighter and Still Can't Get Laid

There is one perk about being a firefighter. And no, it isn't running the risk of being burned alive, rescuing a cat in a tree, or watching a child turn to ash right before your eyes and knowing that you can do nothing to stop it. Sure, those are all pretty cool, but nothing compares to the fact that every chick fantasizes about having you put out *their* fire—you know, the one burning from deep within the walls of their vagina.

But with you, eh, not so much. WTF?

The WTF Approach to Getting F*#!-ing Laid

> **STEP #1: *Clean Your Uniform***

Jesus Christ, that thing is nasty. Don't you ever wash the dirt and grime and blood off that thing?

> **STEP #2: *Burn Your Face Off***

You might as well start over, with a new, fresh face. Burn off the grotesque piece of flesh you call a face the next time you're face to face with a ball of flames.

> **STEP #3: *Get a Better Job***

Being a fireman is great and all, but if you're not the sexy fireman type then you're going to have to make more cash to woo women. The uniform isn't cutting it, time to try an expensive Italian suit.

Sexiest Professions

FOR MEN	FOR WOMEN
Fireman	Dominatrix
Cop	Stripper
Surfer	Porn star
Doctor	Whore
Pool boy	Librarian

Least Sexy Professions

FOR MEN	FOR WOMEN
Manny	DMV clerk
Creepy guidance counselor	Meter maid
Tollbooth operator	Tollbooth operator
Coal miner	Well-educated, successful anything
Grave digger	Judge Judy

70. You Drive a School Bus but Hate Kids

The children sing the entire ride to school. One day, you've had enough: "The wheels on the bus go round and round, round and round, round and round. The wheels on the bus go round and round all . . ."

"Shut the fuck up!" you scream at the little animals, whose downright childish stupidity has finally, after months of torture, driven you totally and completely insane. One little pussy, Billy, cries, while the others just stare quietly, scared out of their wits. For the rest of the drive they actually shut up.

But the next day it's back to normal. That's right, no matter how terrible and mean you are, these kids just will not get the message and act like adults. Bastards!

The WTF Approach to Dealing with F*#!-ing Kids

➤ **OPTION #1: *Invest in an iPod***

Listen to your favorite, upbeat songs to help drown out the sound of the children's horrible voices and put a smile on your face. Naturally, you'll have to still look at them once in a while to make sure they are safe and you don't get sued, but at least you won't have to hear every inane comment they make.

➤OPTION #2: *Throw Them Under the Bus*

Literally. Just toss the troublemakers under the bus and run over them. Not enough to kill them, but enough to show them who's boss.

➤OPTION #3: *Ditch 'em*

Leave them stranded in the middle of nowhere. If Option #2 is a little too harsh, just drive them out to an open field, park the bus, take the keys, and leave the little fuckers. Maybe hide out and watch them lose their shit, just for fun. Eventually one of them will take the lead, à la *Lord of the Flies* . . . that would be better than any reality show on television.

for the ladies . . .

You should never be in this position. You're genetically designed to *love* children no matter what. If for some reason you can't stand kids, you should go to your doctor immediately because you probably have a brain tumor . . . or a very, very small dick.

WHAT THE F*#! IS UP WITH . . .

WORKING WITH KIDS YOU HATE

Why do many people who choose to work with kids hate them? The mean schoolmaster, the uptight bus driver, the fascist gym teacher—the only staff member in school who likes kids is the typically avuncular kind-hearted guidance counselor. The reason? He is a sexual deviant steps away from prosecution.

WTF: UP CLOSE AND PERSONAL

I had a bus driver in grammar school that I hated. She was a total bitch. Then one day she surprised me by agreeing to play my George Michael tape, particularly the song "I Want Your Sex," which I found to be very, very cool since it kept repeating the word "sex." Luckily, she did not actually want my sex, since, to be honest, overweight middle-age bus drivers with bad skin and hair like red wool were not (and are still not) my type. Three cheers for Ms. Whatever-the-fuck-her-name-was.

—GB

71. You Knock Out a Customer with a Bottle

You should have realized this wasn't *Cocktail*. And that you are no Tom Cruise. The two of you have nothing in common. He looks good playing air guitar in his underwear, you don't. He is rich and famous, you're not. He is a clinically insane idiot, you're . . . well, you might have *that* in common.

Nonetheless, part of your job as a bartender is being able to show what a prodigious juggler you are, tossing glasses in the air like a side-show attraction. And you were doing pretty well too, until you got cocky and tossed a bottle of Grey Goose in the air while spinning around to catch it. That didn't work out so well. In fact, the bottle fell on a customer so hard you nearly killed him. WTF?

The WTF Approach to Handling a F*#!-ing Bleeding Customer

➤ OPTION #1: *Buy the Guy a Drink*

It's the least you can do. Give him a few shots on the house for the pain. Assuming he does not have to be rushed to the hospital, that is.

➤ OPTION #2: *Get Drunk*

Before the guy wakes up and sues the shit out of you, take a few bottles and leave the premises. It might not help him any, but at least you'll feel better about the whole thing.

➤ OPTION #3: *Join the Crowd*

Laugh along with everyone else at this poor schmuck lying on the floor in a pool of his own blood.

➤ OPTION #4: *Ignore It*

That's right; he's not the only person in the bar. Odds are nobody even saw it—or gives a shit if they did. All those losers in the bar care about is getting *their* drink, so get back to work. Let his friends deal with him.

for the ladies . . .

Just giggle and say, "Sorry." Push your tits out too when you say this. Works every time.

IN THE FUTURE . . .

Practice makes perfect. Study Cruise's moves at home. Practice throwing bottles in the air like a jackass while watching *Cocktail*.

Worst Things to Get Hit in the Head with . . .

1. Another person's head

2. A baseball bat

3. Your father's fist when he comes into your room after another one of his "nights"

4. A dick

5. A dick with herpes

Best Things To Get Hit in the Head with . . .

1. Jennifer Lopez's ass

2. Pamela Anderson's tits

3. A hundred dollar bill falling out of the sky

4. A snowball (remember, now you can take revenge and throw it back . . . harder)

5. A soccer ball that ricochets off your noggin and into the goal

72. You Work in Fashion Retail but Are Colorblind

"Excuse me, sir. Does this shirt go with these pants?" "Does the brown wash me out?" "Do you really think that these pink jeans look masculine?" These are the kinds of questions you get every day at your job. Usually you can wing it, but it's getting harder everyday. Turns out you are slightly color-blind and didn't even know it. It is only a matter of time before someone at work notices—and you're out of a job and back on the street . . . which is usually gray by the way.

The WTF Approach to Seeing like a F*#!-ing Dog

➤ STEP #1: *Act Confident*

Pick out outfits for your customers with energy and confidence, and you should be good. When the customer questions why you would pick out a hot pink shirt, a fire-engine red pair of pants, and a baby blue baseball cap just tell them that "mixing colors is trendy." All you have to do is say some-

thing is trendy and any moron will buy it.

➤ STEP #2: *Switch Specialties*

When you finally get found out, start working at a tuxedo shop. You can't go wrong there. Just tell anyone who wants to buy a tuxedo that is light blue or any other color besides black or white that he is a tacky pig and then throw him out of the store. Seriously, what is this the '70s? Can you imagine James Bond wearing a baby blue tux? Of course not. If black and white are good enough for Bond, they should be good enough for any far less attractive man. That means *you*.

➤ STEP #3: *Quit Retail*

And become a seeing-eye person. Let's face it, you have no business being in that business. You'll be a big hit as a seeing-eye person (like a seeing-eye dog) for the blind. Think about it. Not only can you see like a dog, you can talk and communicate with the blind person much more effectively than even the most well trained canine.

WHO NEEDS COLOR ANYWAY?

It's a fact that many animals don't see color. Popular belief is that when a bull sees the matador waving the red cape it becomes crazed and attacks. Truth is they just get pissed that an obviously flamboyant gay man is waving a sheet in their faces . . . everyone knows bulls are homophobic.

WTF ABOUT TOWN

We wanted to know what it's like to not differentiate between colors. So we found this colorblind guy on the street. The following conversation ensued.

WTF: What color is my shirt?

Colorblind Guy: I don't know.

WTF: Ha ha! He said he "doesn't know." Ha! What color are my pants?

Colorblind Guy: Again, I really don't know. I can't differentiate between colors well because I am colorblind.

WTF: You're kidding. You really can't tell? Ha! They're blue dummy. Blue! Ha!

Colorblind Guy: I'm going to go now.

WTF: Wait, hold on. We have a joke for you. Ready?

Colorblind Guy: Go ahead.

WTF: How can a colorblind guy tell if he is feeling blue?

Colorblind Guy: How?

WTF: The retail salesperson tells him. Get it? Ha!

73. You Flood the House When You Try to Fix a Leak

Way to go, shit for brains. All you had to do was fix a small leak in your client's kitchen, just like your dad taught you when you were a kid. Remember going with him to work when you were little? Remember how he said that you would "never make it in the plumbing business" and that you were a "born loser" and that he wishes you "never set foot in this world"? Well, now that you are standing in four feet of water, it seems that dear ol' dad had a point. Loser!

The WTF Approach to Saving Face After a F*#!-ing Flood

➤ OPTION #1: *Swim Away*

Swim out the front door and never come back. In fact, leave town and start up another in what will surely be a series of failed plumbing business ventures. Maybe you aren't a total dumbass, but you just aren't a good plumber. Maybe you're *too* smart for this job, the way Einstein was too smart to locate a decent barber. Go back to school for theoretical physics. It's worth a shot.

➤OPTION #2: *Blame a Black Guy*

It's an unfortunate reality in our racist society that every time a white person does something wrong they tell the authorities that an African American is to blame. Say some big black guy in a hooded sweatshirt pushed you out of the way and caused a flood. Take some stuff from the house to make it look like a robbery. To make it more believable, also say that the black guy yelled something about Hurricane Katrina when he busted the pipes, and that he said that this was "just the beginning," an omen of future floods at white peoples' homes to come.

NOTE: You will be contributing to the continuance of racist stereotypes and the consequential persecution of African Americans by doing this, but it's better than paying for all your client's destroyed furniture. Make sure to give to an African-American charity when you get some cash.

➤OPTION #3: *Drown Yourself*

Your father was right; you have no place in this world. End it now and save yourself and your family from future embarrassment.

Things to Do During a Flood

* Round up all the animals on an Ark and get them to bang

* Play Dead Man's Float . . . except for real

* Blame George Bush

WTFACT: Think you caused a lot of damage? Check out the death toll of the top three worst floods in U.S. history:

1. Johnstown, Pennsylvania (1889): 2,200 dead

2. Mississippi Valley (1937): 1,100 dead

3. Santa Paula, California (1928): 450 dead

74. You Are a Plumber and Can't Keep Your Pants Up

You are plumber, your father was a plumber, his father was a plumber, his father was a plumber . . . in fact, you can trace your proud plumber's roots all the way back to the Middle Ages. And just like all the great plumbers before you, you have an uncanny ability to fix a sink, but you're sense of dress leaves something to be desired. In fact, your dirty jeans barely cover half of your lily white ass.

The WTF Approach to Keeping Your F*#!-ing Pants up

➤ **OPTION #1: *Rock It***

You're a plumber, not a fashion icon. Wear your jeans proudly around your ankles and show that crack off! Hot!

➤ **OPTION #2: *Stuff It***

Wear big white underwear. Pull those Fruit of the Looms up to your belly button and, if neces-sary, tie a string tightly around them to hold them in place. It's gross, but it's better than flaunting your hairy ass and scaring your client's children.

➤ **OPTION #3: *Wear a Thong***

Might as well make showing your crack hip and hot, rock a leopard-print thong and show that baby off.

You'll be the most professional-looking plumber out there. So what if you get a little piss and shit on your double-breasted coat. It's good for business—and nothing a little dry cleaning can't take out.

WHAT THE F*#! IS UP WITH . . . SHOWING THE CRACK

Crack kills! It used to be reserved for plumbers, but now it's for everyone. Girls, guys, small children: the hip thing now is not to sag baggy jeans like the hip-hoppers of old, but to sag tight jeans. Everywhere there are hipsters with jeans so tight that they look like leggings. All around the country penises and testicles are being forced into a tiny pair of designer denim, with a space in the back for the crack to show. This can be hot for girls, but not for dudes. Seriously, guys, buy some comfortable jeans and pull them up—no one wants to see your flattened bulge and the tip of your ass crack. Well, almost no one anyway.

WTF ABOUT TOWN

We talked with one of these poor, flattened bulges in Silver Lake, Los Angeles, a hipster's paradise, and a bulge's hell.

WTF: How are you?

Bulge: How am I? What are you a fucking idiot? I'm flattened like a fucking pancake, man. I can't fucking breathe! I got to get out of here! WTF?!

WTF: Relax, bulge. I know a kid that needs a bulge right now. He wears really baggy pants and sags the shit out of them.

Bulge: Really?! Oh my God! The thought of all that freedom of movement brings me to tears. I miss that. I once filled in for a bulge of a whirling dervish in Iran for a few months. Man, that was amazing. Total freedom, brah.

WTF: Cool.

chapter eight

work place
emergencies

75. While Fixing a Telephone Line You Cause a City-Wide Blackout

You knew this wasn't your day from the moment you woke up. Hungover and possibly still drunk from the night before, you would've called in but you have no more sick days. Really, what could go wrong though? You just need to repair a couple of telephone lines, and call it a day. Then it happens, you accidentally straddle some wires and fry your balls off. And if being a ball-less freak weren't bad enough, you cause a major blackout in the process. Good work, no-balls!

The WTF Approach to Dealing with a F*#!-ing Blackout

> **OPTION #1: *Start a Riot***

Sure riots can be scary, but they always look like a little fun on television. And with no surveillance or security systems working you could steal some good shit. Then right before it gets out of hand

fix the problem and save the day. Yeah you!

> **OPTION #2: *Leave Town***

Eventually everyone is going to find out that it was you. You'll forever be known in town as the jack-

ass who made the city go black.
So pack your shit and leave. Don't
tell anyone where you're going.
The people will say, "Hey remember Charlie? He disappeared the
day of the big blackout." People
will remember you and mourn
you for years.

➤ OPTION #3: *Own It*

Make a public statement that
you were the one who started
the blackout and that you did it
to protest the amount of electricity we use. Tell the public that we
should go back to the old days
when people read around a fire
and talked to one another instead
of going in their rooms, getting on
their laptops, and watching hardcore pornography.

> **WHAT THE F*#! IS UP WITH . . .**
> ### WIGGING OUT DURING A BLACKOUT
>
> Everyone makes such a big deal when
> blackouts occur. So there are no lights,
> so what? Was there a riot? Did anyone
> die? Was anyone raped? No, then not
> interested.

WTFACT: One of the worst blackouts in
U.S. history was the New York City blackout
of 1977. The blackout lasted over twenty-four
hours, and resulted in massive looting and
arson. In all, 1,616 stores were damaged,
1,037 fires were called in, and 3,776 people
were arrested. On the upside, the notorious
Son of Sam killer was scaring the city half to
death. Good times.

Things to Do During a Blackout:

- Steal

- Pillage

- Plunder

- Steal, pillage, and plunder

- Look at the moon

76. You Work at a Nuclear Plant and Cause a Nuclear Leak

Good job Homer Simpson. Remember when they told you not to drink Jack Daniels straight from the bottle during work hours? Well, maybe now that you have caused a nuclear fallout that will result in the premature deaths of hundreds of thousands of people from radiation poisoning, you finally know why.

The WTF Approach to Spinning a F*#!-ing Nuclear Fallout

➤ OPTION #1: *Confess*

You know, like George Washington did to his father after he cut down the cherry tree. You'll probably lose your job, but at least you'll know that you did the right thing. This fact should be comforting to all those kids suffering from radiation poisoning on account of your dumb ass.

➤ OPTION #2: *Brag About It*

Use the accident to become famous. Okay, infamous really. Go on *Oprah* and tell the world that you are sorry. Write a book about what a moron you are and what a disaster you caused. Confront your victims on *The Tyra Banks Show*. Sure, you will be hated. But at least you won't be an unknown nuclear power plant operator any-more. You'll be a star!

► OPTION #3: *Make a Political Statement*

Tell the press that you did this intentionally in order for Americans to feel what the poor inno-cent people did in Hiroshima and Nagasaki after we nuked their asses. You might face criminal charges, and most Americans will hate the shit out of you, but at least you'll be thought of as a calculat-ing terrorist, rather than just a moron.

WTFACT: On April 26 1986, a reactor exploded at the Chernobyl plant in the Soviet Union, releasing 400 times more fallout than was released after the bombing of Hiroshima.

Also in 1986 . . .

- Space Shuttle Challenger explodes, killing seven astro-nauts. Seven-year-old WTF? author Gregory Bergman makes a joke about the accident. Grandfather makes him feel so guilty about the joke that he still feels like a shithead to this day.

- *Oprah Winfrey Show* airs for the first time.

- Michael Jackson was still black . . . sort of.

- U.S. bombs Libya. Gaddafi still pissed.

- Ronald Reagan was still an asshole.

77. You're a Doctor and Mix Up Your Patients' Charts

You graduated at the top of your class in medical school. You have built a successful practice and are one of the most sought after brain cancer specialists in the state. But even you can make mistakes. Unfortunately, in your profession, a mistake can actually kill someone. You should have been a dentist, asshole. Instead, you're now a murderer. What to do when you mix up a chart and tell a patient he has allergies when he's actually got a tumor the size of a baseball in his fucking brain?

The WTF Approach to Recovering from a Huge F*#!-ing Mistake

➤ OPTION #1: *Apologize*

Call him up and tell him you are sorry. If a grieving widow answers and informs you that he has "passed on," hang up immediately and move your practice to another state.

➤ OPTION #2: *Own It—Sort Of*

Leave a note on his car. If it works good enough when you bump into a parked car, there's no reason it isn't sufficient for gravely misdiagnosing someone, potentially resulting in their otherwise preventable death. Make sure not to write too sloppily or they might know the writer was a doctor and trace it back to you.

➤ OPTION #3: *Ignore It*

Throw away the chart. Sure, it's not the most ethical thing to do, but neither was being a fucking idiot and putting the patient in danger. Lord knows you went into medical school to make money, not help people. So keep your trap shut and let him die.

GREAT DOCTOR JOKE

A man goes back to the doctor after undergoing some tests a couple days before. The doctor calls him in and says, "I have good news and bad news. Which do you want to hear first?"

"Tell me the good news."

"You have twenty-four hours to live."

"That's the good news?! What's the bad news?"

"The bad news is I tried to call you yesterday."

Medical Laughs

"My psychiatrist told me I'm going crazy. I told him, 'If you don't mind, I'd like a second opinion.' He said, 'All right. You're ugly too!'"—Rodney Dangerfield

78. You Crash into Your Boss's Car

There you are late for work again. You cruise down the freeway at 100 mph and fly into the company lot. You look at your watch. Whew, just in time. You'll be able to get to your desk without anyone noticing you're late. You turn the corner and then—*wham*—you slam into the rear end of your boss's Mercedes. WTF?

The WTF Approach to Getting Away with Wrecking Your Boss's F*#!-ing Car

➤ OPTION #1: *Pass the Blame*

Park your car very far away and start running. Then when you're good and sweaty run into the office and tell your boss you just saw some asshole hit his car and take off. You, being a good citizen, chased after the car, but it got away. You'll look like a hero for chasing after the car. You might even get a raise. Use the extra funds to fix your car.

➤ OPTION #2: *Start Crying*

Walk into the office crying like a baby. Tell him you are very sorry and that you will take care of it. Pussy.

➤ OPTION #3: *Drug Him*

Drop some sleeping pills in his coffee. When he passes out take him to his car and drive him somewhere out of the lot. When he wakes up he'll think he blacked out while driving and hit something. He'll probably be in a panic, thinking he has a brain tumor or some shit like that, but fuck it, not your problem.

> **OPTION #4: *Flip the Switch***

Blame that pompous ass for the crappy parking job. What did he expect leaving his car parked like that? It was only a matter of time before someone hit it.

Get to Work on Time

If you are constantly late for work, we suggest the following changes to your routine:

- Use a jet to get to work, not a beaten down Pinto that doesn't start.

- Wake up earlier. If you have trouble waking up, stay up all night drinking Red Bull.

- Carpool with people who are not lazy morons like yourself— you'll be forced to get up in time.

- Pluck your eyebrows at night, rather than in the morning. And by the way, any dude that plucks his eyebrows is gay.

- Jerk off at night. Yes, a good jerk in the morning is splendid; we'll give you that. But there is a time and place for everything— including ejaculating all over yourself.

Water Cooler Talk

"I once hit into my boss's car, but I never told him. He passed me up for a raise two years in a row. Now that's fuckin' karma!"

—Kevin Tahl, accountant

79. You Spill Coffee on Your Computer

Fuck! Shit! Goddammit! Son of a bitch! Oh, for Christ Sake! Motherfucker! Not again! Jesus!

Yep, you've done it again, jackass. You spilled coffee all over your keyboard, monitor, and some even dripped into the processor. And forget about your pants, your penis hasn't been this hot since what's her name gave you your first—and her first—painfully inadequate hand job in the seventh grade. While you can probably save the computer, your work from today including that important assignment is now kaput. FUCK!

The WTF Approach to Dealing with a F*#!-ing Coffee-Soaked Computer

➤ **OPTION #1:** *Start a Witch Hunt*

Go to your boss and complain that some idiot came into your cubicle and knocked over your coffee, and didn't have the damn decency to fess up to it. By the end of the day he'll be interrogating everyone, and will have long forgotten about that pressing assignment, buying you a couple more days.

➤ OPTION #2: *Clean It Up*

What the fuck are you doing just sitting there with your hands on your head, rocking back and forth and lamenting over your stupid mistake and your lost work? Clean it up, dipshit!

➤ OPTION #3: *Suck It Up*

Literally. It is wrong to soak it up with a paper towel when there are starving people in China who would love a cup of coffee to fill up their empty stomach. Get on all fours and slurp it up.

WTF: UP CLOSE AND PERSONAL

I have spilled coffee on my work computer and personal laptop over 7,000 times in my life. To tell you the truth, I like it.

—GB

WTFACT: Over 99 percent of the working population has spilled coffee or another liquid on their computers. The remaining 1 percent is made up of camels and people who are so fucking anal they make you sick.

WTF ABOUT TOWN

WTF: Excuse me. What would you do if you spilled that cup of coffee on your . . . (*WTF* loses footing and knocks into the schmuck, causing his coffee to spill onto his lap and all over his computer.)

Random dickhead worker: AAAHHH!! What the fuck?!

WTF: Well, that answers my question.

Things You Should Never Spill Hot Coffee On

* Your crotch . . . unless you're into pain
* Your car dashboard
* Crack
* Small children
* Your wife's tits . . . unless she's also into pain

80. You Smoke a Cigarette in the Bathroom and Set Off the Sprinklers

Smoking is bad for you, but being a moron is worse. You just had to have that cigarette didn't you? Well, as smokers ourselves we understand the need. But go outside or take a quick puff and flush it, dipshit.

The WTF Approach to Enduring a F*#!-ing Office Rainstorm

➤ STEP #1: *Take a Stand*

We smokers are persecuted enough as it is, confess to what you have done and give an inspirational speech about smokers' rights. You might lose your job, but you'll be remembered as a hero.

➤ STEP #2: *Quit Your Job*

Give up your promising career in advertising and become a laborer on a construction site. At least you can smoke outdoors . . . sometimes.

➤ STEP #3: *Quit Smoking*

Get clean and healthy and become one of those annoying ex-smokers. Make sure to tell smokers that you quit because you are such a fucking hot shot. You might not have friends, but at least you'll be able to walk up a flight of stairs without an oxygen tank.

WTF: UP CLOSE AND PERSONAL

Every time I am on an airplane, I smoke. In the bathroom, with the toilet seat up, I take a couple drags and toss it in the shit sucker. One time a stewardess (I refuse to call them "flight attendants") said the bathroom smelled like smoke after I left, and accused me of being the culprit. I told her that I noticed a smell too, and it must have been the person before me. She prodded, saying it was me. I then emphatically told her I don't smoke and my father died of lung cancer—a total lie.

The point is that, with no proof, you can always deny it unless someone sees you smoking.

—GB

A SMOKE FEE SOCIETY

Sin taxes are shameful. Taxes on soda, cigarettes, and beer—the three major American food groups. A pack of cigarettes now costs an arm and a leg, like in New York where they can cost up to $10 a pack. This will not make people quit smoking, it will just make them broke.

And not to mention you can't smoke anywhere anymore. In Santa Monica, California, you can't smoke anywhere in the whole town. This is bullshit. We smokers have given you the airplanes, restaurants, even the bars. But do you really need the whole fucking town? In some states the law now is that you are only allowed to smoke in your house, in a closet, with a friggin' blanket over your head.

Smoke 'em while you got 'em, because sooner or later you won't be able to!

Who Smokes What?

Match the smokers to their favorite substances to smoke:

1. Tobacco Pipe
2. Pot

3. Cigarette in long cigarette holder

4. Cigar
5. Peyote

A. Sarah Palin
B. Old man with white beard in corduroy jacket reading book in study
C. Fat guy in business suit in strip club

D. Old movie actress or drag queen
E. Hunter S. Thompson

ANSWER KEY

1. B; **2.** E; **3.** D; **4.** C; **5.** A

side
jobs

81. You're a Waiter but You're a Total Klutz

>>>> Being a waiter is the oldest profession in the world next to being a prostitute, but it's far more degrading. That said, you can make good, fast money if you work in the right restaurant. After landing a gig in a top restaurant, you soon realize that a winning personality and a good memory for orders isn't everything: You also have to be able to walk five feet without dropping something. In one shift you've managed to break a half dozen glasses and drop a bowl of pasta on someone's lap. A 20 percent tip is definitely out of the question—and so is keeping your job.

The WTF Approach to Stop F*#!-ing Tripping

> **OPTION #1: *Take a Ballet Class***

Ballet is a great way to increase balance and flexibility. Unfortunately, it's also a great way to look like a fairy.

> **OPTION #2: *Get Help***

Pay someone to carry your food. Tip the bus boy a little extra money for taking your food to the table. If they don't speak English, then just make them do it without paying them. They'll never know the difference. There just happy to be alive.

➤ OPTION #3: *Work at a Greek Restaurant*

They like to break dishes and glasses. It's how they celebrate. You'll fit right in. Everyone will just assume you are the life of the party. *Opa!*

Other Things Popular in Greece

- Sleeping with livestock
- Having hair all over the face, back, and neck
- Feta cheese, pita, and olives
- Ouzo
- Metaphysics

You Might be a Klutz If . . .

❑ You can't go three steps on flat ground without putting your arms out to regain your balance.

❑ You can't change a light bulb without electrocuting yourself.

❑ You can't take a shit without falling in.

❑ When you do the waltz, it looks like you're break dancing.

❑ Every time you jerk off on a tightrope you fall.

for the ladies . . .

You might be a klutz if every time you try to insert your tampon in your special lady hole it winds up in your mouth.

82. You're a Drug Dealer but You Keep Smoking the Weed

So you have a great job selling drugs. Way to aim high . . . literally. You have one of the few positions with job security; people will want your product no matter what state the economy is in. One problem though, you want it too . . . bad.

The WTF Approach to Keep from Smoking Your F*#!-ing Stash

➤ **OPTION #1:** *Start Selling Crack*

You'll make way more money and be able to support your weed habit.

➤ **OPTION #2:** *Go Corporate*

Get a job at a medical marijuana clinic in California. Hey, it's legal and, like most retail, you probably get an employee discount.

➤ **OPTION #3:** *Hide Your Stash*

Do it during the one hour a day you aren't stoned off your ass. Careful though, you don't want to lose a sale because you can't find the goods.

➤ **OPTION #4:** *Become a Reggae Singer*

You already have the weed habit, now all you need is a Che Guevara T-shirt, a stupid hat, and filthy dreadlocks. Oh, and practice your Jamaican accent too.

Places with the Best Employee Discounts

* Clothing store

* Pharmacy

* Bar

* Jewelry store

* Brothel

Places with the Worst Employee Discounts

* Sperm bank

* Nuclear plant

* Morgue

* Sanitation dump

* Bed, Bath & Beyond

Stoner Aptitude Test

Need help figuring out what career path to take, pothead? Answer these questions.

1. What kind of work is most conducive to being stoned?

    A. Heart surgeon

    B. NASCAR driver

    C. Fighter pilot

    D. Food tester for Frito Lay Corporation

2. What kind of work is least conducive to being stoned?

    A. Rock star

    B. Video game developer

    C. Graphic designer

    D. Mountain climber— without a rope

ANSWER KEY

1. D, jackass
2. D, jackass—do it! We dare you!

83. You're a Prostitute and You Undercharge

L ook, times are tough and sometimes you got to do what you got to do. While you might not have always dreamed of entering the world's oldest and most disgusting profession, looks like the fantasy of being a ballerina didn't exactly pan out the way you thought. And not only that, you aren't even making much money doing it. You're a whore and you're not making any money. WTF?

The WTF Approach to Being a Better F*#!-ing Prostitute

➤ STEP #1: *Market Yourself*

Facebook, Fuckbook, Suckbook . . . get on the Net and post the best pics you've got. Announce specials like the back-to-school sale, the holiday special, and "Fuck a Rabbi for Free Tuesdays"—or something like that. If you build the buzz, they will cum.

➤ STEP #2: *Get Bigger Tits*

People always pay more for big tits. It's a law of the universe. This is especially true for you dudes; trannies fetch a high price.

Fresh and Clean

In the legal and regulated brothels of Nevada, not a single brothel prostitute has contracted HIV since 1986 when mandatory testing began. That means banging one of these broads is about a million times safer than banging some chick you met at a cocktail party. Food for thought.

➤ **STEP #3:** *Specialize*

You might not get as many clients but the ones you do get will pay through the roof. Specialize in domination, submission, and, if you really want to make the big bucks, let your client shit on your face. Yes, it's gross. But then again, so is being a dirty whore.

84. You Work Security in a Graveyard and Are Afraid of the Dark

Some men are brave. Some men conquer their fears. Some men can handle any situation. And then there are pussies like you. When you got a job doing security at a graveyard you figured your childhood fears wouldn't haunt you—now that you are thirty. But, they still do. Bitch.

The WTF Approach to Fighting Your F*#!-ing Fear

➤ OPTION #1: *Throw in the Towel*

Seriously, if you're a grown-ass man and you're still afraid of the dark, then you have bigger problems. If you can't, then there is no good reason why you should live in a world of men. So curl up in the fetal position, suck your thumb, and cry yourself dead.

➤ OPTION #2: *Get a Really Big Flashlight*

You know the old saying, the bigger the flashlight, the bigger the pussy. At least now you will have a nice big light that will not only make you feel safe, but also deter anyone from coming around who shouldn't be there.

➤ OPTION #3: *Bring a Friend*

Come on, who doesn't want to hang out in a creepy graveyard at three in the morning? Start by asking your Goth friends. Careful, if they raise the dead you could lose your job.

COMMON PHOBIAS

Fear of the dark is a common phobia; here are some other things that other pussies are afraid of:

- Arachnophobia: Fear of spiders
- Aerophobia: Fear of flying
- Claustrophobia: Fear of small spaces
- Acrophobia: Fear of heights
- Necrophobia: Fear of death (not to be confused with necrophilia, which is more fun and less scary)

NOT-SO COMMON PHOBIAS

- Aulophobia: Fear of flutes
- Unattractiphobia: Fear of ugly people
- Hippopotomonstrosesquippedaliophobia: Fear of long words
- Metrophobia: Fear of poetry
- Dildophobia: Fear of a dildo getting shoved up your ass
- Sciurophobia: Fear of squirrels (. . . getting shoved up your ass)

Phobias in the Making

These new phobias are taking the nation by storm.

- **Twitterphobia:** Fear of getting Tweeted

- **Starbuckaphobia:** Fear of seeing a fucking Starbucks no matter where you are

- **Realityshowphobia:** Fear of turning on the TV and only seeing losers eating bugs for money

- **Michaelvickaphobia:** Fear of Michael Vick stealing your dog for his gruesome dog fights

- **Brangelinaphobia:** Fear sweeping parents throughout the Third World that any more of their kids will be stolen by these lunatics.

85. You Gain Twenty Pounds While Working at a Fast Food Restaurant

One of the benefits of working at a fast food establishment is getting to eat the food for free. Before long you are seriously addicted to fast food, and crave nothing else. Fries, chicken nuggets, burgers, milkshakes—your disgusting habit begins to overwhelm you. Then one day you go to bend over and your muffin top belly pops the button on your pants. Maybe they shrunk in the wash . . . or maybe you gained twenty pounds, fat ass!

The WTF Approach to Dealing with F*#!-ing Weight Gain

➤ OPTION #1: *Keep Going*

Why stop at twenty? Keep getting bigger and you might develop diabetes or a heart condition. When that happens, you could have a lawsuit against the company. Imagine how many cheese-burgers you could buy with $1 million?

➤ OPTION #2: *Embrace It*

Smear the fries on your face. If you are going to be a fat fuck, you might as well be a pimple-ridden fat fuck. People will feel even sorrier for you. Go on Match.com and try to meet a hot dermatologist chick. Women are always looking to "change" the men they are with. Maybe they'll consider your repulsive skin and hanging stomach a worthy challenge.

➤ OPTION #3: *Become Bulimic*

This way you can continue eating the shitty foods you love while keeping your figure. Sure your teeth will start to rot in your head and your breath will stink, but if you're eating all that fast food to begin with, your breath probably smells like ass anyway.

➤ OPTION #4: *Get Colonics*

Next to putting your finger down your throat, this is the fastest way to lose weight. You go there, they pump your colon full of laxatives and out comes those burgers, fries, tacos, burritos—even that birthday cake from 1987. Yum!

You Are What You Eat

Calorie burning calculator: See what burns what . . .

ACTIVITY	CALORIES BURNED
Basketball (60 min.)	558
Reading (30 min.)	30
Archery (25 min.)	136
Sex—foreplay (10 min.)	16
Sex—intercourse (30 min.)	144
Sex—with a donkey (45 min.)	300 (for the girl); 400 (for the donkey)

86. You're a Pizza Delivery Boy and Deliver a Pizza with a Slice Missing

Nothing is more tempting than the smell of a fresh pizza, the scent of tomato sauce and greasy cheese emanating from the cardboard box next to you. Your senses tantalized and your belly growling from hunger, one day on your way to your next stop you break the code every pizza delivery boy is sworn to uphold: Don't eat the fucking pizza, fat ass. Fuck, before you know it the twelve-slice large pepperoni pie has been reduced to eleven pieces. How the hell are you going to explain this one?

The WTF Approach to Covering Up the F*#!-ing Evidence

➤ OPTION #1: *Say You Were Carjacked*

Tell the customer that you are very sorry but that it isn't your fault. You were carjacked by a gang member and pizza enthusiast at gunpoint. Heroically, you grabbed the gun from his hand and threw him out of the car—but not before he grabbed one slice. You put your life on the line to save the hot, fresh pizza you have sworn an oath to deliver.

> **OPTION # 2: *Say You Gave It to a Homeless Person***

Tell the customer you are so sorry but that on your way you saw a homeless child missing an arm holding a sign that said, "Hungry for pizza, spare a slice . . . please!" You know that it wasn't your slice to give away, but when you see that kind of sadness in the world you must, as a good Christian, do your best to help the less fortunate. They'll be so moved they might just forgive you.

> **OPTION #3: *Come Clean . . . Sort Of***

Tell them you ate the slice but that, in your defense, you are a diabetic and would have gone into a coma had you not eaten something. Again, if you are convincing, they might just let you slide.

WTF: UP CLOSE AND PERSONAL

Before I was the author of the best-selling *WTF?* series, I was a humble pizza delivery boy. Eighteen and a freshman in college, I didn't have much work experience—and it showed. I was constantly lost and, when I finally did deliver the pizza, it was often cold. But, I managed to get by due to my innate charm and fabulous personality. Then, just when things were going well, my car broke down and with it I lost my job. Luckily I had gained over twenty pounds in three months working as a pizza delivery boy because, every time an order was messed up, we all got to eat the pizza so it wouldn't go to waste. Unemployed and starving, I lived off my excess pizza fat for over two months before I was forced to move back in with my mom. Come to think of it, this is not a funny story at all, but a sad commentary on the lonely and unstable life of a pizza delivery boy. I see an incredibly somber and moving memoir in my future.
　　—GB

87. You Work as a Landscaper but Are Allergic to Pollen

You wanted to be a rock musician or a ball player when you were a kid. But inevitably you failed miserably and at thirty years old, with no education, you had little choice but to take over your father's landscaping business. One problem: You are extremely allergic to pollen and just about anything that's green. Flashbacks of mowing the lawn dripping snot all over yourself as a child haunt you as you try desperately to deal. But it's just too much for any one man to bear.

The WTF Approach to Coping with Your F*#!-ing Allergies

➤ OPTION #1: *Get Allergy Shots*

If Claritin doesn't cut it, get some allergy shots. They hurt a little, but a tough landscaper like you should be able to handle it.

➤ OPTION #2: *Wear a Mask*

This will protect you from pollen. Sure it might not be a good look to draw the ladies, but then again, neither is mowing a lawn in a filthy T-shirt sweating like a pig. On second thought, maybe we are wrong—that does sound kind of hot.

➤ OPTION #3: *Move*

There are places with no pollen, like the desert. Move to Vegas and specialize in desert landscaping—designing front yards with cacti and rocks and shit. Don't let a little thing like allergies get in the way of your dreams, however stupid they might be.

HEADHUNTER'S TIP

Don't be a landscaper . . . loser.

Worst Things to Be Allergic To

- Air
- Pussy
- Chocolate
- Cement

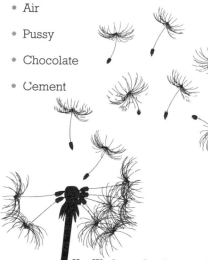

IN THE FUTURE . . .

Be born of strong stock with genes that can withstand a little flower's pollen. Pussy.

getting
fired

88. You Want to Quit but Need Unemployment

It's official. You hate your job. Every *fucking* thing about it. You hate your boss. You hate your coworkers. You hate your desk. And you really hate that stupid inspirational picture on the wall of a rock with a caption that reads "Perseverance." Fuck perseverance. But you can't just quit and forgo unemployment benefits. WTF?

The WTF Approach to Getting F*#!-ing Canned

➤ OPTION #1: *Do Nothing*

If you stop showing up, the company might be able to rightfully deny you unemployment. But if you just sit there like a fucking dunce, you should be safe. Just stare at the computer and zone out all day, every day until they can't take it anymore.

➤ OPTION #2: *Fake a Mental Breakdown*

You're on the verge of a real one anyway. Start flipping out screaming and then hold your head and rock quietly at your desk. Who knows, before they let you go they might even suggest some paid time off. A vacation could do you some good. True, the vacation will probably be in an institution, not the Bahamas, but it still beats sit-

ting in that fuck-
ing cubicle all
day surrounded
by people you wish
were dead.

➤ OPTION #3: *Fall Down the Stairs*

Break a leg or
another useless
bone (when was
the last time you
went running,
anyway?), then
take some paid
time off and get
some workman's
compensation.
It's better than
unemployment
and eventually
could lead to
disability—the
American
dream.

You Might Be Getting Fired If . . .

❑ Your boss is watching every
move you make.

❑ Your coworkers start to avoid
you.

❑ Your password doesn't work.

❑ You hear rumors about the
company merging.

❑ You're a moron and it was
just a matter of time.

Top Reasons Someone Gets Fired

Dishonesty and/or a bad attitude

Employer: This is great work.

Employee: Go fuck yourself!

Refusing to follow directions and orders.

Employer: I want this report by Friday

Employee: I want a lot of things in life. What's your point?

Lying on a resume.

Employer: It says on your resume you speak the Southern African tribal tonal language of Xhosa fluently.

Employee: Yes I do.

Employer: So do I.

Employee: Shit.

Talking too much and conducting personal business at work.

Employer: Is that report done yet?

Employee: Not yet, sorry 'bout that.

Employer: Why not?

Employee: I've been updating my Facebook status all day. It's very time consuming. Hey, why didn't you add me as a friend?

Inability to actually do assigned job tasks.

Employer: I need you to staple these presentations together.

Employee: Not a problem. How do I work the stapler?

89. Your Company Suddenly Relocates Without Telling You

At first when you show up at the office and the lights are off you think everyone is throwing you a belated surprise birthday party. But after fifteen minutes you realize not only is no one there at all but all the offices have been locked. The phones are dead; the computers are gone. Then it hits you, your company has vanished, just like in that movie *The Game*. But, unlike Michael Douglas's character, you're a broke loser and you're now out of a job. And by the way, if it took you fifteen minutes to realize that there were no desks, offices, or people, then it's no wonder they left your stupid ass behind.

The WTF Approach to Picking Up the F*#!-ing Pieces

➤ OPTION #1: *Collect Unemployment*

Technically you have been fired, but without the notice and severance pay. So drag your ass over to the unemployment office and start getting some cash. Then go get drunk. On second thought, get drunk first then go to unemployment—just like most of the pigs in line.

➤ **OPTION #2:** *Burn the Building Down*

Start the fire, then call 911. Tell them you came to work and found it like that. The authorities will find those bastards for you.

➤ **OPTION #3:** *Start Your Own Company*

You have the space, now fill it. Get a bunch of investors, hire a bunch of people, and promise them equity, and then split, leaving everyone with their balls in their hands. What goes around comes around.

COMPANIES THAT SHOULD VANISH

It would be a better world if these companies simply disappeared suddenly.

- ShamWOW
- Wal-Mart
- AIG (before we gave them trillions of dollars)
- Halliburton
- The Olive Garden

Water Cooler Talk

"I came to work one day and found that the whole office and everyone had vanished. I thought I was on like 'shrooms or getting punked for a second but they actually did disappear. Luckily I work for my father and I hate him with all my heart. Fuck you, dad! Free at last!"

—Ted Johnson, unemployed with serious daddy issues

90. You Get Fired for No Good Reason

It starts like any other day. You wake up with your hand on your dick, you get your medium nonfat triple shot vanilla twist homo latte, and head to your cubicle, ready for yet another day at the grind. When the boss asks to "see you for a minute" you figure it must be about that project you're working on. Instead, he just says two words: "You're fired!"

And that's it. One second you're gainfully employed, and the next second you're worrying about paying the bills. Pleading for an explanation, your boss just tells you that if you don't leave in five minutes he'll call security. That's right; you've just been fired for no reason. WTF?

The WTF Approach to Life After Getting F*#!-ing Canned

➤ OPTION #1: *Investigate*

Someone is responsible for this. Put some feelers out, bribe people for information, follow home coworkers you suspect of wrongdoing, and, if necessary, interrogate these suspects using controversial tactics such as water boarding, pulling out eyelashes, and playing Barry Manilow's "Copacabana" at an ear-piercing volume over and over again.

➤ OPTION #2: *Fuck It*

Hey, as long as they give you unemployment, who gives a shit why they fired you. Take some time off to work on your music career. If you can't play an instrument, being out of work should provide you with ample time to learn. By the way, chicks love a guy who can play the guitar . . . start carrying one around and you won't have time for work because you'll be getting so much pussy!

➤ OPTION #3: *Stalk Your Boss*

Call him on his office, home, and cell phone until he finally comes clean and gives you the reason for your termination. If he gets a restraining order against you instead, you might want to consider the same controversial tactics as described in detail above in Option #1. Not for information, but just for a few laughs.

The Five Stages of Firing

Here's how to apply the five stages of grief in this WTF moment . . .

Stage #1: Denial

Boss: You're fired.

Employee: This can't be happening to me

Boss: It is.

Stage #2: Anger

Boss: Now get the fuck out!

Employee: I am going to fucking rip your face off and hang it from my rear view mirror.

Boss: SECURITY!

Stage #3: Bargaining

Boss: Leave.

Employee: No.

Boss: Yes.

Employee: I'll suck your dick.

Stage #4: Depression

Boss: You're fired. Just go.

Employee: That's fine; my life isn't worth living away. (Puts gun to head.)

Stage #5: Acceptance

Boss: Be a man. You're fired. Now leave.

Employee: That's cool . . . I'm gonna learn how to play the guitar and get tons of pussy . . . starting with your wife's.

Top Five Ways to Get Fired

1. Sell office items on eBay.

2. Walk around the office with your pockets out and your cock dangling from your open zipper.

3. When your boss enters your office while you are on the phone, quickly wrap up the call with, "I'm gonna have to call you later. The J - E - W is back."

4. Sneeze blood. Don't clean it up.

5. Punch people.

91. Your Wife Gets Laid Off the Same Day You Do

The whole way home all you can think about is how you are going to tell your wife that you were let go. Will she be pissed? Will she be comforting? Will she divorce you and marry someone who *isn't* a loser? These are the questions that plague you as you pull into the driveway, walk up the door of your soon-to-be-repossessed home, and, reluctantly and with a deep sigh, walk in to face the music. Then you see her in kitchen sitting at the table, her face buried in her hands. You exhale and decide to just blurt it out, "Honey, I have bad news. I got laid off today."

She looks up, tears in her eyes. "You're fucking shitting me. So did I!"

The WTF Approach to Making F*#!-ing Ends Meet

➤ STEP #1: *Blame One Another*

"How could you get fired?" "Oh yeah, how could *you* get fired?" And so on and so forth. The most adult thing to do in this situation is to blame the other person until the situation is magically resolved.

➤ STEP #2: *Have Sex*

Soon you'll be thrown out of your house and onto the street, enjoy a good make-up romp in your comfortable bed for the last time.

➤ STEP #3: *Renew Your Vows*

You might have to wait until you are both gainfully employed to do this properly, but renewing your vows is a must. Obviously you two losers are perfect for one another. Inject new life into your relationship and live happily ever after—in the homeless shelter.

➤ STEP #4: *Sell One of Your Kids*

The little blond boy will fetch a fair price.

WTF UNEMPLOYMENT QUIZ

1. Have you looked for work this week?
   A. Yes, everyday.
   B. Yes as much as I can.
   C. Why, is it lost?
   D. What day is it?

WTF UNEMPLOYMENT QUIZ—*CONTINUED*

2. What resources have you used to look for work?
   A. Internet, paper, temp office
   B. Job postings in Starbucks
   C. Friends and family
   D. My bong

3. What kind of work would you be willing to do?
   A. Anything, I just need a job.
   B. Something that doesn't involve hard labor or typing.
   C. Something that pays a lot for a little work.
   D. Eating, drinking, sleeping, or banging. I'm really good at all those. Well not really the last one. But you get my drift.

ANSWER KEY

1. A
2. A
3. A

NOTE: If you answered B or C or D to any of the above questions or even considered it you are a scumbag who does not deserve to work—or to live—in these beloved United States.

92. You Have a Jerry Maguire-Style Breakdown and Nobody Joins You

You knew you shouldn't have written that mission statement. Now you're being canned. But that's alright because you are going to start your own company—a company based on principles like fairness and justice, a company that's not just about numbers, but about people.

"Who's with me?" you shout with open arms to the blank faces. But despite your impassioned speech, nobody, not even a desperately horny single mom to a mongoloid child is willing to join you. Now, with no job and no prospects, you're on your fucking own. Shit!

The WTF Approach to Going F*#!-ing Nuts

➤ **STEP #1:** *Tell Everyone to Fuck Off*

You might as well. As you walk out tell everyone to shove it and then tell everyone that your new company is going to put them out of business.

➤ STEP #2: *Grab the Goldfish*

At least the fish will come with you if no human being will. They are your only friends now, so make sure not to over feed them.

➤ STEP #3: *Start Laughing*

Stop your screaming and pretend you were just joking. Tell everyone you recently joined an Improv group and this was one of your homework assignments. Funny, right? You probably won't get your job back, but at least no one will think you're a lunatic.

Most Famous Breakdowns

- Sir Isaac Newton
- Michael Richards
- Britney Spears
- Amy Winehouse
- Gary Coleman (well not yet but he should—what a little loser)
- Sinead O'Connor

IN THE FUTURE . . .

Make friends, asshole. If you had some true friends at work they would come with you.

93. Your Coworker Gets You Fired

Thanks a lot, asshole. And to think you bought this bitch lunch one day, remember that? Now this little piggy returned the favor by getting you fired! You knew you shouldn't have told her that you weren't actually sick last week, but instead decided to take a much needed vacation from your boss, whom you hate. Well, the gig is up and your boss knows that you weren't home in bed after all. Why? Because bitch-face told him, that's why!

The WTF Approach to Life After Getting F*#!-ing Fired

➤ STEP #1: *Ask Why*

Like a dying man in a movie killed by his best friend, confront her and ask, "*Whyyyy?!*" This will probably only make you look insane and weak but who cares? You'll never see these assholes again anyway.

➤ STEP #2: *Get Revenge*

Get your coworker fired. Call in the office using different voices every day asking for her and, if she isn't there, tell the receptionist to tell her that she is a whore. Order a ton of pizzas for delivery to the office under her name, slash her tires in the morning so she's late for work, and find any other creative way you can to make her life miserable and put her in the spotlight at work. Eventually, whether it's her fault or not, the bosses will can her for being a nuisance.

➤ STEP #3: *Join a Cult*

Since you'll likely lose your house now that you're worthless and unemployed, you need to get a roof over your head. Most cults give you a place to live as well as three squares a day. Cults offer better conditions than prison or a homeless shelter—though you'll be surrounded by really dangerous people.

➤ STEP #4: *Become a Stand-up Comedian*

Start hitting the clubs and talk about how this asshat at work got you fired. Tragedy + Time = Comedy . . . this shit will be funny. Then publicly name this person every time you get on stage. Eventually it will get back to your coworker.

for the ladies . . .

If this happens to you, find that coworker's husband/boyfriend and sleep with him. If she's not dating anyone, go find her father and screw him.

WHAT *NOT* TO DO

• Kill her

Everything else is fair game.

94. You Are Denied Unemployment

etting fired is bad enough, but getting fired and then being denied unemployment—the one thing to keep you going—is just about the worst thing that can happen to a person, except perhaps a vicious herpes outbreak. Then again, if you have ever been given the boot and then denied unemployment benefits, you might take ass herpes over it any day—though employers never give you that choice. In all seriousness, not being able to make ends meet is a scary fucking prospect.

The WTF Approach to Getting Some F*#!-ing Money

➤ **OPTION #1: *Fight It***

Go to the appropriate agency that handles unemployment benefits in your state. Just Google "unfairly denied unemployment benefits" and you should be directed to all the relevant info. If you cannot Google "unfairly denied unemployment benefits," then you prob-

ably were not "unfairly" denied anything, moron.

➤ **OPTION #2: *Beg***

Listen, the fact that you were fired for jerking off at your desk wearing nothing but a pinwheel hat and flippers does not exactly bode well for you in that unemployment hearing. The state won't side with you—no matter how liberal it is. You're best just calling your boss and begging him for the benefits. Make sure to promise to pay him back later when you get another gig.

➤ OPTION #3: *Threaten Sexual Harassment*

No matter what you did to get fired, legal or illegal, you can always threaten to sue for sexual harassment—even after you worked there. If you won't win the unemployment hearing, you might as well make some cash at your former employer's expense some other way.

WTF: UP CLOSE AND PERSONAL

I was once denied unemployment after I purposely got myself canned from one of most horrible jobs in the history of work as an editor of a financial magazine. The bastards I worked for then denied me unemployment without any basis other than their misplaced adolescent anger.

Without a dollar to my name and a wife to support, I needed this unemployment to survive. So I fought it—and won. I was not only granted unemployment but also an additional settlement the specifics of which I cannot discuss. But I can say that I did not get that blowjob I asked for in the initial agreement. Fucking lawyers; they ruin everything!

—GB

WTF? Work *Quiz*

1. In most states, which of the following is *not* a valid reason to deny a terminated employee unemployment benefits?

   A. Caught performing sexual acts with the boss's stapler

   B. Never showed up for work

   C. Set the warehouse on fire

   D. Because the boss is a scumbag

2. What is the best thing about receiving unemployment benefits?

   A. You don't have to get up to go to work.

   B. You don't have to stay late at work since you are never at work.

   C. You get paid to smoke pot and watch *Star Wars* all day.

   D. All of the above

3. What is the worst thing about being unemployed?

   A. When you hear on the news about the unemployment rate, you know you are part of it.

   B. Filling out that questionnaire every week or so about the jobs you supposedly queried.

   C. Friday nights and Happy Hour lose their meaning and appeal.

ANSWER KEY

1. D
2. D
3. B (Really, those things are just too time consuming.)

chapter eleven

starting
over

95. No One Is Hiring

You're finally out of school and ready to enter the job market. One problem, there is no job market. That's right, you have just entered the worst economy in the last fifty years. Due to the circumstances, you're even willing to start at the very bottom as long as it's a good company. But then you find out that the only place hiring in your town is the Taco Bell and being an actual citizen, you're shit out of luck there too. WTF?

The WTF Approach to Dealing with a F*#!-ing Shit Economy

►OPTION #1: *Go Back to School*

Stay in as long as you can so you have an excuse for being unemployed. Maybe by the time you get out the country will have its shit together.

►OPTION #2: *Become an Actor*

These people never have a job. If you say you are an actor waiting for that perfect role no one will question why you are so broke.

➤ OPTION #3: *Become a Criminal*

Rob a bank or a liquor store, start making and selling meth, or pirating CDs and DVDs. If you get away with it long enough you might be able to make some serious cash and move to Mexico. We hear it's a really safe place for drug runners to retire.

➤ OPTION #4: *Start Your Own Business*

Invent a service or product that no one needs and make some money. Think of the pet rock or more recently, the Snuggie. That jerk off just invented a backwards bathrobe and charged $19.95. Shit, even you could do that.

Great Business/Product Ideas

If you do want to start your own business or invent a new product, here are some good ideas we came up with to get your brain going.

Carwash for Homeless People: Homeless people might not have the money for an apartment with a shower, but that doesn't mean they wouldn't pay a few bucks to get clean. Imagine a carwash-type set-up with a moving walkway like the ones at the airport, except with shackles so the homeless person's feet are secured. In five minutes these dirty bastards will look like new.

Piggy-Bank Bank: Remember putting change in your piggy bank as a kid? Piggy banks are fun; everyone likes them. Start a chain of banks shaped like a piggy bank, with escalators on the sides that lead to an opening at the top from where the customers will enter. You'll put Bank of America out of business in no time!

Goldtooth: It works like a Bluetooth, but with a gangsta twist. Just like a fake gold tooth, it sits in the front of your mouth. Using your pinky finger, just tap the Goldtooth to make and receive calls. It's da bomb, yo!

96. You Are Forced to Live with Your In-Laws

Everything was going so well. You just moved into a new apartment with your wife, and things were really starting to come together. But then the unthinkable happened: You and half your department got laid off. Now you are unable to pay rent and have no place to go—except one: Your dreaded in-laws house. Fuck!

The WTF Approach to Living with Your F*#!-ing In-Laws

►OPTION #1: *Put on a Happy Face*

Make sure to feign interest in everything you father-in-law says. He may be a senile moron, but part of the job as son-in-law is nodding and pretending to be fascinated in whatever the old man has to say. Agree with every outdated and silly idea he has, no matter how much you object to them. There's no reason to argue with him; you'll never change his mind. You might, however, get the opportunity to change his diapers —if you're into that shit.

►OPTION #2: *Lay Down the Law*

If you sense a weakness in your father-in-law, slowly take charge of the household, usurping the old patriarch's power. Sit at the head of the table, take control of the channel changer, and send the old man out back to rake the leaves.

Once you become the boss, you'll have no reason to leave.

► OPTION #3: *Make Yourself Useful*

If you aren't man enough to pull off Option #2, better get your ass in gear. Help your mother-in-law wash the dishes, shine your father-in-law's shoes, and just in general be everyone's bitch.

> **WHAT THE F*#! IS UP WITH . . . FEARING YOUR FATHER-IN-LAW**
>
> In movies, books, television—and even in real life—men are always being portrayed as being scared out of their wits when meeting their girlfriend's dad. But why? Who the hell is this clown anyway? Why is it your job to impress him? Instead of trying to prove that you are a good guy, he should be trying to prove that his daughter—despite blowing you within half an hour of your Match.com date—is really a good girl at heart.

Remember . . .

Screw quietly. Cover your wife's mouth when you bang her so her father doesn't hear. He may be eighty years old, but he still knows his way around a shotgun.

Water Cooler Talk

"When my wife and I first got married I was out of work so we decided to save money and move in with her parents. I really wasn't thrilled about it at first but I told myself it would only be for a short time. One night while her parents were out of town we decided to have some long overdue, wild sex. My wife is very vocal and since we were living with her parents she had to tone it down, but this night we let loose. We were in the hot tub going at it like teenagers, and she was screaming, 'YES! More! Harder, Daddy!' And I'm like, 'Yeah, I'm your daddy.' And then I heard a voice behind me: 'No,' the man said. 'I'm her daddy.' Turns out her folks had come home early. We moved out a month later."

—Rich Mollar

97. Your Coworkers Get a Better Severance Package Than You

Getting fired sucks, but most of the time if you are let go you get a decent severance package, a little cushion for you to enjoy while you look for another job. So when you and some of your coworkers got the boot you tried to look on the bright side. Then you get the news: You ain't getting shit—but they are. WTF? You were all let go at the same time and you've been at the company longer than most of them. This is some serious bullshit!

The WTF Approach to Getting Your Fair F*#!-ing Share

> **OPTION #1: *Fight It***

Go into your boss's office and demand to know why you received nothing. Careful though, he might then rattle off all the ways you fucked around while working for them and how you should be grateful to receive unemployment, let alone a cushy severance pack-

age. If this happens, humbly thank him for his time and slink out of there with your tail between your legs.

> **OPTION #2: *Sue***

If you don't have a case, make one up about sexual harassment. Worst-case scenario, they will settle out of court and give you what you deserve.

➤ OPTION #3: *Rob One of Your Coworkers*

Break into his place and steal some shit. Sure that kind of karma is bad but if you received less money to begin with you probably already have bad karma, so who gives a shit? Make these jerks share the wealth.

➤ OPTION #4: *Take What's Rightfully Yours*

Make your own severance package. If you didn't get what you deserve then take it, bitch! Steal a computer, fax machine, or your boss's car. They owe you.

for the ladies . . .

This is an easy one. Plant a hidden camera in the bathroom and film yourself taking a piss. Then have a friend post it on the Internet. You can sue for millions—and get famous at the same time!

WTF News: Severance Packages Getting More and More Pathetic

With the economy in a mess, it's no surprise that employers are cutting back on severance packages in a big way when they give you the boot. In fact, here are some of the severance packages that major corporations are now offering their employees.

- **Lehman Brothers:** A coffee mug that says: "I did *not* survive the bailout of 2009!"

- **Cigna Health Insurance:** One year policy of Cigna Health Insurance. Not a bad deal unless you actually get sick.

- **Wal-Mart:** A warm smile and a handshake followed by a polite, "You're fired. Now get the fuck out of here!"

- **General Motors:** An American car . . . yuck!

98. You Have to Move In with Mommy

Pat yourself on the back. You've been on your own since you were eighteen; never looking back after you left the nest and made a place for yourself in the big, wide world. But now, at thirty, you've lost your job and with it the apartment that you have called home for years. With nowhere else to turn, you pack up and go back to the house you grew up in, your head hanging low in shame. WTF?

The WTF Approach to Living with F*#!-ing Mommy

➤ **OPTION#1:** *Keep Your Room Clean*

Sorry, but Mom's house, Mom's rules. You remember the drill. Keep your room clean or you won't get any supper. How's that for being humbled, huh? What's that? You better watch your mouth! One more peep out of you and you're going to have your mouth washed out with soap! Go to your room now, you little asshole!

➤ **OPTION #2:** *Revert to Childhood*

Drink all your mom's booze, sneak out at night, and make a fucking mess in the kitchen every time you go in there. At first, your mom might be pissed, but deep down she'll be happy that her little shitty son is back, just the way she remembered you.

➤ OPTION #3: *Don't Take Shortcuts*

Now that you are older you see how much work it is to keep a house, let alone support someone. This time do your chores the right way. When you sweep the floor, don't sweep the dirt and dust under the rug, the way you used to. When you rake the leaves, don't just dump them in the neighbor's yard. And when you jerk off all over yourself in the bathroom, don't just wipe yourself down with the guest face towel just because it's easier than using a few wads of toilet paper. Also, don't wait for her to ask you for help. Take some initiative, you ungrateful piece of shit!

WTF: UP CLOSE AND PERSONAL

At twenty-five years old, I was forced to move back home with my mother after years of independence. I didn't really mind, but she did. I was a pig, and did not help out enough. I am deeply ashamed of myself. May God have mercy on my soul.

—GB

BEST THINGS ABOUT LIVING WITH MOM

- Free food
- Free rent
- Free booze
- Free laundry
- Free *everything*

WORST THINGS ABOUT LIVING WITH MOM

- Hearing your mom having sex

That's it . . . is there anything worse?

Dealing with Mommy Dearest

How to use living with your mom to your advantage.

Girl: Let's go to your place.

Guy: Okay, but I live with my mom.

Girl: What? Oh my God! Then maybe we shouldn't . . .

Guy: I live with my mom because she's mentally ill and I have sacrificed part of my life to take care of her.

Girl: Oh my God! That is *so* sweet. You're amazing. I want to sleep with you right now.

Guy: Great. My mom would appreciate this.

99. You Lose Your Will to Live

After being laid off, rehired at another firm, and then laid off again, you realize that living on the streets isn't for you. You are weak, pathetic, and you know it. You want to reach out and get some much needed support from your friends, but no one wants anything to do with a loser like you. After years of barely making it, you hit rock bottom and lose your will to live.

The WTF Approach to Picking Yourself F*#!-ing Up

➤ OPTION #1: *Be a Man*

Pull yourself up by your bootstraps. In other words, don't be a fucking pussy, pussy. Take charge of your life and make some moves. If you really are a born loser, find an ugly rich broad to live off of. Smoking pot and eating cereal all day on someone else's dime may not be the best way to spend your existence, but it's better than checking out completely.

➤ OPTION #2: *Join the Armed Services*

If you are suicidal anyway, you might as well go out a hero. We need more people in this country willing to sacrifice their lives. God will also let you into heaven if you fight for your country.

➤ OPTION #3: *Kill Yourself*

This is an obvious option, considering you now believe that life—at least *your* life—is not worth living. If you think this, you are probably right. End it all right now. Seriously, bro, do it!

> **WTF LEGAL:** If you do kill yourself, we are not responsible. Well, not legally, anyway. Good luck on the other side, bro!

To Be or Not to Be?

Should you really kill yourself? Take this quiz to determine whether or not your life is worth living.

1. Are you actually taking this quiz to determine whether you should kill yourself?
2. Do you have a disgusting wart on your face that cannot be removed surgically?
3. Are your average Friday and Saturday nights very similar to your average Monday night?
4. Do you only have one ball and are not a famous cyclist?

5. Was Bill Clinton president the last time you got a blowjob?
6. Are the number of dollars in your bank account less than the number of inches of your dick?
7. Do you have an extra leg protruding out of your skull?
8. Do you take what the pundits at Fox News say as gospel?
9. Is your only true friend a ball with a face drawn on it like Tom Hanks in *Cast Away*?
10. Do you make under $100,000 per year *before* taxes.

Answer Key

• If you answered "yes" to two questions (especially #9) you need therapy but shouldn't kill yourself just yet.

• If you answered "yes" to three questions just end it.

• If you answered "yes" to five or more questions you won't have to wait to kill yourself—we're already on our way to do it for you.

100. The Only Work You Can Find Is Volunteer Work

You are getting plenty of job offers, which is a good thing now that you're out of a gig. The only problem is that these jobs don't exactly pay the bills. In fact, they don't pay at all! What to do when the only work can you get is volunteer work.

The WTF Approach to Getting F*#!-ing Paid

► **OPTION #1: *Be a Mensch***

Okay, so you might not get paid in the traditional way, but how can you compare this paper thing called money used to exchange for goods and services with the warm, fuzzy sensation that you get from helping humanity?

► **OPTION #2: *Fuck the World***

Just like that Biggie Smalls song. Time to look out for numero uno, bro. When you've got rent taken care of then you can start fooling around with volunteer shit.

► **OPTION #3: *Start Selling Drugs***

Sell some crack or meth on the side to make some extra cash. Shit, most of the volunteer organizations are for needy, homeless people who are probably addicted to drugs anyway—you'll have a built in clientele. Win, win!

The Most Famous Givers

People a lot better than you have devoted their lives to improving humanity throughout history. Here's a list of the most giving and caring superstars:

- Mother Teresa

- That fat guy with the white beard in those Christian charity commercials asking for "Just 70 cents a day"

- Angelina Jolie and Brad Pitt

- Jack Nicholson's character in *About Schmidt* who adopted that African kid

- Harriet Tubman (unless she secretly charged a fee to ride the Underground Railroad)

- That cute girl in 6th grade who gave you your first hand job . . . God bless her!

101. You Are Forced to Live on the Streets

You figured you'd get another job after your unemployment ran out. Well, you figured wrong, dick wad. Now, after losing your unemployment insurance, your girlfriend, and the tiny sliver of pride you were desperately clinging to, you are forced to move from your cozy apartment in the suburbs to downtown's skid row.

The WTF Approach to Living like a F*#!-ing Animal

➤ OPTION #1: *Move*

Listen, we know that places like Manhattan and Hollywood are more happening than rural Oklahoma, but it's better to shack up in a nice, comfy double-wide in a field somewhere than sleep like a jam-packed sardine in a homeless shelter downtown. If you are in a place that is beyond your means, go Croyhound and get the fuck out of dodge.

➤ OPTION #2: *Make Them Drag You Away*

Stay as long as you can until they drag you out. If you don't have the rent, don't just pack up and leave. It takes months for a landlord to evict you. Change the locks, and wait it out until the cops break the door down. When they pound on the door, go James Cagney on them. "You'll never get me copper!" Then laugh maniacally and wait until the men in white coats take you away to the loony bin; it beats jail and the shelter.

➤ OPTION #3: *Embrace It*

It's nice to get back to nature and live off the land. No credit cards, no phones, no television influencing every decision you make. Think Henry David Thoreau in *Walden*.

Advantages to Living on the Street

- Plenty of room

- Constant change of scenery

- Wherever you go you're home

WTF: UP CLOSE AND PERSONAL

While I was in college, my roommate moved out suddenly, leaving me to pay the rent all by myself. That was bad enough, but after my car broke down, I instantly lost my pizza delivery job, as well as transportation to look for another. Feeding myself was now a challenge, let alone paying rent. I was starving. I used up whatever cash I had and bought ten dozen eggs in bulk for a discount. I had eggs for breakfast, eggs for lunch, and eggs for dinner. Within a week I had literally started to turn green.

Sick to my stomach and wont of a better life, I sat at home every night, ignoring the eviction notice on the door. Though the landlord desperately pounded on the door and tried to open the lock, the sofa and chair I used as a blockade remained secure (I could not afford to change the locks). I had created a little fort from which I could plot my escape. Eventually, I found someone to stay with. As a final "fuck you" to the landlord, I left him the piles of garbage that had accumulated during the three weeks I spent without leaving the apartment.

And that's how I roll, dawg.
—GB

WTF Career Aptitude Test

Well, we've come to the end of our little journey together. Hopefully, you've learned a little something about navigating life in the workplace. But before you know which particular kind of corporate prison you want to slave away in for the rest of your life, take this test to find out a little more about yourself.

Multiple Choice

1. When you have to work with someone who has bad breath you . . .

   A. Offer them a mint or gum

   B. Hold your breath

   C. Hold their breath

   D. Ask them politely if someone took a shit in their mouth

2. When your boss asks you to stay late you . . .

   A. Think "Go fuck yourself" but say "Great!" in your usual cowardly way

   B. Say, "Go fuck yourself"

   C. Beat him mercilessly about the face, head, and neck with a stapler

   D. Explain to him that you are a werewolf, and that in the interest of everyone else's safety, you really should go home

3. Friends would describe you as . . .

   A. A leader

   B. A follower

   C. A stalker

   D. A tranny

4. Which of these are you more likely to volunteer to participate in?

   A. Local blood drive

   B. Actor in a local play

   C. Wingman for your horny friend

   D. I don't volunteer, asshole

5. Which outfit is NOT appropriate for working in a day care:

   A. A Chippendales costume

   B. Lame sweater vest—Mr. Rogers–style

   C. Button up shirt

   D. Your favorite crotch-less jeans

6. When entering a crowded party, what is your natural tendency?

   A. Do something to become the center of attention.

   B. Get wasted and vomit in someone's purse.

   C. Find the drunkest girl in the room and try to get her to go home with you.

   D. Scream "Fire" then video everyone running for their lives.

7. You have a tendency to:

    A. Always think before you act.

    B. Always act before you think.

    C. Masturbate before you think

    D. Eat pizza more than twice a week

8. When asked to help with your friend's party, which task do you select?

    A. Vomit cleaner-upper

    B. Semen cleaner-upper

    C. Vomit, semen, and blood cleaner-upper

    D. MC

9. Others see you as . . .

    A. Logical

    B. Impulsive

    C. Ambitious

    D. Hung

10. When explaining something, you . . .

    A. Go into lots of details and facts

    B. Draw stick figures

    C. Stutter then start to cry

    D. Explain it once, and if they don't get it then tell them to go fuck themselves

11. In conversations with strangers, you typically . . .

    A. Talk more than they do

    B. Talk less than they do

    C. Talk about the same amount as they do

    D. You do not talk to strangers because they might kill you

12. You would rather have . . .

    A. An exciting job

    B. A fun job

    C. A high-powered job

    D. Any fucking job

13. In a high-pressure situation, you . . .

    A. Stay calm and think of a logical solution

    B. Shit your pants—a lot

    C. Sweat like a fat pig so that everyone can see it on your shirt and becomes disgusted by you

    D. Get an erection

14. When it comes to rules, you . . .

    A. Always follow them, even when you don't agree with them

    B. Only follow the rules you agree with

    C. Try to change the rules you don't agree with

    D. Laugh at the thought of giving a shit about anyone or anything other than yourself

15. You are tasked to help launch a new product. Which of these tasks is best suited for you?

    A. Conceptualizing the product

    B. Selling the product

    C. Designing the product

    D. Banging your coworker who developed the product really, really well

16. What do you like least about your current career?

    A. I get bored easily

    B. I wear too many hats

    C. High risk chance of getting an STD

    D. There's not much on television during the day

17. What do you like most about your current career?

    A. The money

    B. I get to be creative

    C. The people

    D. You get to use a gun

18. Which of the following would you consider your primary strength?

    A. Motivating team members

    B. Research

    C. Creative development

    D. Handling several lattes and bagels at once

19. How do you respond in situations where your idea or plan is not working out?

    A. I ask my more intelligent assistant to work on it then take credit for her work.

    B. I examine the plan and find its weak spots.

    C. I commission the help of others to make the plan work.

    D. I drink heavily, and then vomit.

20. Your department must make a group presentation to your company. Which role is best suited for you?

    A. Defining trends in the data

    B. Collecting supporting data and facts

    C. Creating the slides

    D. Sitting there and nod like a total useless jackass

21. Which of these tasks can you complete with the least amount of difficulty?

    A. Pick out the perfect gift for someone

    B. Add large sums in your head

    C. Write a poem

    D. Draw your penis perfectly from memory

22. Your car broke down on the highway and won't start. What do you most likely do?

   A. Kick the car and curse at it

   B. Pray to a God that doesn't exist

   C. Call for a tow

   D. Check under the hood because you're a man and you can fix that shit yourself

23. You're asked to help plan the office's annual party. Which of these tasks do you volunteer for?

   A. Managing the budget

   B. Creating the invitations

   C. Selecting the location and the menu

   D. Bringing the whores

24. If you could be a kid again, which of these activities would sound most appealing to you?

   A. Losing yourself in a video game

   B. Losing yourself in a movie

   C. Losing yourself in a great book

   D. Losing yourself in the babysitter's vagina

25. You are helping your roommate build her dresser. What is your approach?

   A. Let her build it, and help out if asked

   B. Read through the instructions and then start building it

   C. Work from the photo on the box and try to make it look that way

   D. Go down to Home Depot and grab some Mexicans to build it

26. Which of these statements would most likely appear on your resume?

    A. People person

    B. 12-inch cock

    C. Beat *Grand Theft Auto* in one sitting

    D. Mom thinks I am special although there is overwhelming evidence to the contrary

True or False

Are you a workaholic? Read each statement and decide whether it's true or false to see if you are.

27. Your idea of "quality time" with your family is occasionally glancing at their photo on your desk.

    • True
    • False

28. The last time you had a vacation was during the Reagan Era . . . and by that we mean when he was governor of California.

    • True
    • False

29. When the clock strikes 5 P.M. and it's time to leave the office, you start to cry.

    • True
    • False

30. Between sex with a super model and a challenging assignment, you'll take a challenging assignment.

    • True
    • False

There are really no right or wrong answers. Reflect on your answers and take similar psychological tests to more fully understand what kind of person you are, as well as what profession would best fit your personality. And once you know what you would like to do, you can do what everyone else does who is armed with that special knowledge: The exact opposite if it pays more.